*All about
God in Christ*

The "All" Series by Herbert Lockyer . . .

All about God in Christ
All about the Holy Spirit
All the Angels in the Bible
All the Apostles of the Bible
All the Books and Chapters of the Bible
All the Children of the Bible
All the Divine Names and Titles in the Bible
All the Doctrines of the Bible
All the Holy Days and Holidays
All the Kings and Queens of the Bible
All the Last Words of Saints and Sinners
All the Men of the Bible
All the Messianic Prophecies of the Bible
All the Miracles of the Bible
All the Parables of the Bible
All the Prayers of the Bible
All the Promises of the Bible
All the Teachings of Jesus
All the Trades and Occupations of the Bible
All the Women of the Bible

All about God in Christ

■ ■ ■

Herbert Lockyer

HENDRICKSON
PUBLISHERS

© 1995 by Hendrickson Publishers, Inc.
P. O. Box 3473
Peabody, Massachusetts 01961–3473
Printed in the United States of America

ISBN 1–56563–204–4

First Printing — November 1995

Table of Contents

1

HIS AUTHENTICATION

. . . without controversy great is the mystery of godliness . . .
(1 Tim. 3:16)

The introduction Paul gives to his unique summary of the incarnation of Christ, which condensation is deemed to be a fragment of some Christian hymn or creed (a feature common to the pastoral Epistles found in the quotations introduced by the fivefold expression, "Faithful is the saying", emphasizes the validity of the virgin birth. It may prove helpful if we treat the two words—*controversy* and *mystery*—separately.

"Without Controversy"—how strikingly emphatic is this assertion, implying, as it does, that there can be no question about the validity of the truth, namely, that Jesus was God manifested in flesh; and that, because of its genuineness and truthfulness it is entitled to full acceptance by faith. The mystery of how He could assume our created nature may be beyond our finite comprehension, but this greatest event in human history itself is beyond all dispute or doubt. Among the interpretations given of the A.V. phrase, *without controversy*, we have:

"Beyond dispute"

"No one would deny"

"Great beyond all question"

"Confessedly wonderful"

"By common confession."

The idea of a united confession is certainly associated with the original word for *controversy*, which implies by consent of all, or confessedly. Prophets and apostles by common consent accepted the virgin birth as the basis of the Christian Faith. The *And*, introducing Paul's magnificent authentication of the Incarnation, is like a hand linking "the Church of the living God" and "God was manifest in the flesh" together, making them one. As Ellicott's *Commentary* expresses it: "*And* is not simply copulative, but heightens the force of the prediction, Yes, *confessedly great is the mystery*—for the glorious truth which the Church of God pillar-like upholds is none other than that stupendous mystery, in other ages not made known, but then revealed—*the mystery of Christ*, in all His loving manifestations and glorious triumph. Yes, confessedly great—so great that the massive grandeur of the pillar is only in proportion to the truth it supports."[1]

The Incarnate Christ could declare, "Abraham rejoiced to see my day; and he saw it, and was glad" (John 8:56). Under the inspiration of the Spirit, hundreds of years before Christ was born, Isaiah added his quota to the confession, "The Lord himself shall give you a sign; Behold, a virgin shall conceive, and bear a son, and shall call his name Immanuel" (7:14. See 9:6, 7). John opens his Gospel with statements affirming his agreement with the historicity of the incarnation of his Lord. "He came . . . " (1:11); "he gave power" (1:12); "the Word was made flesh, and dwelt among us (1:14. See 17:8). This basis of our faith is further authenticated by all the apostles, principally by Paul who, with boldness, makes it plain that he accepted, without any hesitation or apology, the glorious revelation that the Babe of Bethlehem was God manifested in flesh, and that His incarnation was vindicated by the Holy Spirit and by angles (1 Tim. 3:16).

There is the apostle's remarkable testimony to the humility, as well as the fact of the Incarnation in his marvellous description of Christ, as being equal with God yet assuming the form of a slave being born in the likeness of men (Phil. 2:6–8). He became the *outward-fashion* of God all men could see. "I came down from heaven," Christ affirmed, and voluntarily assumed our humanity that He might die as the sinless

---

[1]Charles John Ellicott, ed., *A New Testament Commentary for English Readers* (New York: Cassell, Petter, Galpin, [1878?]–1884).

Substitute for sinners. To this authoritative statement we can add the further Pauline language of Christ becoming a partaker of our flesh and blood in order to destroy the power of the Devil (Heb. 2:14–18). Rich in glory, he became poor on earth, that all who are saved by His grace and power might, through His earthly poverty, become enriched by His mercy (2 Cor. 8:9).

What about our Lord's virgin birth? One trembles when he comes to examine the criticisms levelled at it, because they not only seek the destruction of the miraculous, and of the very foundation of our gospel revelation, but such unworthy and unwarranted criticisms shamefully dishonor our blessed, adorable Lord. For the help of young believers we offer the following summary trusting that it will strengthen their faith in this wonderful descension of Jesus.

Past Criticisms

From the earliest days of the Christian church the virgin birth has been bitterly opposed by men of learning and religious thought.

The Ebionites

This particular sect of early Jewish Christians was not regarded as being among the real body of Jewish Christians because they held that the Mosaic law was binding on Christians; they denied the apostolate of Paul; and they rejected the virgin birth. For these three important matters they remained outside the recognized Christian church until the days of Jerome.

These Ebionites held that Jesus was a man, naturally born, and not the "offspring of a virgin's womb." They recognized, of course, that He was above the ordinary man in that He resembled the Spirit-led man or prophet of Old Testament times, but with all such endowment He was still a mere man who sprang from human parents. And such a view has passed into the thinking of many today. The "Ebionite," being dead, yet speaketh.

These men of the early days possessed a gospel based on Matthew's from which the story of the virgin birth was absent. But such was a spurious copy, a mutilated and corrupted form of Matthew's gospel.

The Gnostics

This sect was prevalent in Paul's day. They are possibly referred to in Colossians 2:18–19, where he seeks to warn the believers at Colosse against their mystical heresies.

The word "gnostic" comes from the Greek word *gnostikos* which means, "Good at knowing." And so these gnostics were the "know-alls" of Paul's day; that is, they presumed to know after the order of a "fleshy mind" more than the revealed truth of God such as the apostle was declaring.

In respect to Christ they allegorized away His person and work. They held that He possessed two forms, one called Jesus, born in a natural way, and another called Christ, which became His at His baptism, and which indwelt Jesus until just before the cross, when the Christ part went back to heaven, and the Jesus part that was left died upon the cross.

Keeping this teaching in mind, one is enabled to understand the Epistle to the Colossians more clearly, for Paul's purpose in writing the Letter was to counteract this error of false mysticism. In a masterly way the apostle shows that our Lord "is not two Beings (Jesus and Christ) somehow united, nor two persons with two minds, two wills, two conflicting existences, wedded in impossible bonds; but one being, harmonious, symmetrical, consistent—not God in man, or God and man, but the God-man." Would that we could hear the apostle's warning of Colossians 2:8 more often than we do!

Present Criticisms

Coming to present-day criticisms and theories, one is appalled to find how general is the denial of the virgin birth of our Lord. It is openly affirmed from the professor's chair, as well as from the pulpit, that your Savior and mine did not come into the world as the Sacred Record says He did, but that He was a man just as other men, and that in respect to His conception there was nothing miraculous. "It will be a perilous day for the Church when," says Professor Orr, "in obedience to the demand of so-called 'modern thought,' the belief in the Virgin Birth is parted with. But we do not believe that, in really faithful circles, that day will ever come." Ah, but apostasy is rapidly spreading, and since Professor Orr's day, many of "the Church" have yielded to the demands of so-called "modern thought" and have parted with their faith in the virgin birth.

Now, to meet the modern apostate view regarding the virgin birth and at the same time confirm our faith, let us classify the objections raised.

The Nonmiraculous Criticisms

The trend of modern thought is to deny everything supernatural and explain all that appears to be of a miraculous nature in the Bible from a natural standpoint. By the process of human reason, the seemingly inexplicable matters are explained as natural phenomena. And so the finding of Professor James Orr is perfectly true in this respect: "The chief cause for the denial of the Virgin Birth of our Lord is the rise and rapid spread of a school of historical criticism which aims at the complete expurgation of the miraculous element from the life of our Lord all through."

Such a method of attack is, to say the least, Satanic, for it weakens the fact of God's omnipotence and also refuses the reliable testimony of the New Testament writers.

The sum of the teaching of this particular school is that of the Ebionites, namely that Christ was an ordinary man after the natural order. As the Creator has decreed that the production of a child can only come by human contact, it is therefore impossible for Him to break the law. But the simple answer of faith is, "Is there anything too hard for the Lord?" He is the Lord of all law, as well as the Lord of all life!

The Documentary Defects

From other sources there is this additional declaration that the virgin birth must be rejected on the ground of its own want of evidence. Now, as there is no adequate reason why an intelligent believer should have any uncertainty as to the verity of this most important fact of our religion, even although its references are meagre in New Testament documents, let us take this objection of documentary deficiency upon its own ground.

1. The Reliability of the Evidence

Perhaps by way of introduction, we may be allowed to quote from a product of "Higher Criticism," namely, *Peake's Commentary*, p. 4: "As regards the birth stories of Matthew and Luke, we find ourselves in doubt on many points, and there is reason to believe that a reverent imagination has been at work on traditional material." Now, this is a very serious allegation, and if true, destroys the validity of the Scriptures, which have been inspired of God, according to the testimony of one writer.

The question before us then is, Can we rely upon the Gospels as being genuine productions? Or are they merely the product of "reverent imagination" woven together out of "traditional material"?

Such a question is important because the writers of the New Testament records were guilty of falsification and gross deception if the contention of the higher critics is proven.

Well, on turning to the Gospels themselves, what do we find? First Matthew and Luke are the only two who give us any account of our Lord's birth and infancy; their united testimony is that He was conceived of the Holy Ghost, and born of the Virgin Mary.

Let us try to prove the orthodox position:

a. These two gospels were genuine documents of the apostolic age.

There is abundant evidence that the early disciples treated Matthew and Luke as genuine documents. For instance, Professor Sanday considers them to be "the oldest and most obviously authentic parts of the New Testament. Their evidence may therefore be accepted without reserve."

b. The virgin birth narratives are genuine parts of these gospels.

In the oldest manuscripts and versions that we have of Matthew and Luke, even although some of these are mutilated in parts, the chapters that recount the virgin birth are to be found essentially as we know them today.

And yet some of the critics discredit the genuineness of these parts, the chief source of their information coming from one named Wellhausen, a German critic, who issued an edition of the Gospels—"translated and explained"—and from which he drops out entirely the story of the virgin birth, giving no note or explanation of his omissions. Why, such a treatment would not be allowable even if a person were dealing with any classical work!

c. The very tests have come down to us in their integrity.

"Here," says Professor Orr, in his monumental work on *The Virgin Birth*, "we encounter a new line of attack. The narrative of Luke is a genuine part of the Gospel, but have we the text in its original form? The evidence of manuscripts and versions as again decisive. Apart from a few various readings such as occur in all texts (the chief of them may be seen in the margin of the Revised Version), the chapters in Luke are vouched for as coming down to us in their integrity."[2] But this evidence does not satisfy some of the critics, and so they set out to delete the narratives in this wise; "Leave out, e.g., verses 34 and 35 of chapter 1"; that is, Mary's question, "How shall this be?" and the angel's answer, which is the crucial verse, "The Holy Ghost shall come upon thee . . . "; and cut out or change a few other clauses, and the story of the virgin birth disappears. You have simply the promise of a son, as in the cases of Isaac, Samson, Samuel, John the Baptist, to be born in the ordinary way, in the estate of marriage. Specially is Luke 1:27, where Mary is twice spoken of as a virgin, to be deleted, and there are some sequential changes. Then, says Hermack: "After these few and easy deletions . . . the narrative is smooth and nowhere presupposes the Virgin Birth." And then, Professor Orr adds, "There is still a difficulty, for, if these deletions are to be made, we should expect notice of the marriage of Joseph and Mary."

2. The Contradiction of the Evidence

Another objection raised is that Matthew and Luke appear to contradict each other in many features, and that such contradiction discredits the truth of the virgin birth. We shall turn again to Professor Orr for an answer to this accusation. He has two points. The first is that the narratives are independent of each other. Matthew does not copy from Luke, nor Luke from Matthew, nor both from a common source.

---

[2] James Orr, *The Virgin Birth of Christ* (New York: Scribner's Sons, 1907).

That is evident from the whole structure of the narratives, and from the so-called discrepancies. His second point is that the narratives are related to each other. Now, all the difficulties raised by the critics immediately disappear when we remember that Matthew and Luke have given their accounts of the virgin birth from different standpoints.

Take Matthew: In his Gospel he gives us the point of view of Joseph, and so you have hardly any reference to Mary. Matthew tells the outward, or public, experiences which follow the facts that came to Joseph's knowledge, and this, it will be found, is in dramatic contrast to Luke's version. There are:

(a) Joseph's perplexity and suspicions (1:19).

(b) His thoughts and purposes (1:20).

(c) His difficulties removed by a divine revelation (1:20).

(d) His gracious, manly, unquestioning response (1:24, 25).

Take Luke: Luke, on the other hand, gives us Mary's viewpoint, and so Joseph is hardly mentioned except as the one to whom Mary was betrothed. As a tender physician, Luke tells us the story of the virgin birth from an inward point of view, as only a physician can, and records experiences which are deeply personal. And so you have:

(a) Mary's call to motherhood (1:28).

(b) Her maidenly fears (1:29).

(c) Her chaste, pure life (1:34).

(d) Her royal submission (1:38).

(e) Her sacred joy (1:39, 56).

(f) Her deliverance (2:5–7).

Now, not only is this relationship observed in the details surrounding the birth of our Lord; it can also be traced in the two genealogies given by Matthew and Luke respectively. It is affirmed that the two genealogies are totally different from each other and bear apparent marks of contradiction. But here again the difficulties disappear as quickly as the morning mist, when we remember the viewpoint of each writer.

Two genealogies there are, because the descent of Jesus is traced along two distinct lines. And, as Dr. W. Choritic points out, all confusion is banished when we remember that "to begin with, the natural answer is that every man has two genealogies, that of his father and that of his mother, and that, even in our own legal matters, cases might arise in which the production of both was necessary." To this there is something of a similarity in the present instance.

Take Matthew: This first Gospel sets out to show the kingly descent of Him who was "born king of the Jews," and so our Lord's royal or legal descent is traced back to King David. In writing for Jewish readers "the gospel of the kingdom," Matthew realizes that it is imperative, at the very outset, "to establish Christ's earthly claim to the throne as the successor of King David."

Take Luke: On the other hand, Luke presents Christ as the perfectly Human One, the Son of Man, that is, as the one who became the Representative Man; and so in his Gospel he lays stress upon His human history, and in the genealogy he gives, he proves the natural descent of Christ by traveling back to Adam.

The Mythical Theories

Other there are who would have us regard the virgin birth as "a late myth which sprang up to account for the impression that the divine character of Jesus made upon His disciples." Such a course is perfectly natural, of course. If one discards the genuineness of the Gospel narratives of the virgin birth, then he must try to explain its existence with such.

Product of Jewish Imagination

According to some critics, the virgin birth is a myth that sprang up on Jewish soil, arising out of the prophetic passage of Isaiah 7:14. But "unfortunately for this explanation, it can be shown to demonstrate that in Christ's time this prophecy was not applied by any Jews to the

Messiah, for the Hebrew word used does not necessarily mean 'virgin' . . . The idea of a Virgin Birth was not one likely to spring up on a Jewish mind at all. It had no precedent in the Old Testament, where high honour is put on marriage (Deuteronomy 22:20, 21). The sons of promise in the Old Testament are all born of marriage."

Product of Gentile Myths

Turning aside from the Jewish origin of the record of the virgin birth, we find newer theories that assert that "the Christians borrowed or imitated pagan myths of sons of the gods, and applied them to Jesus." But such theories are contradicted by the fact that "till the middle of the second century, the Church held itself strictly and uncompromisingly aloof from everything savouring of paganism."

It is useless to spend time discussing such absurd and shameful explanations of the virgin birth for it could be easily shown that there is no comparison between "the lustful tales of the sons of gods in heathenism, in which there is no real instance of a 'virgin' birth, and the simple, chaste, beautiful narratives of the Christian Gospels."

We can afford to leave the matter where Professor Sweet does: "We may with confidence assert that wide excursions into ethnic mythology and folklore have failed to produce a single authentic parallel in fact or in form to the infancy narratives."

Paul made it clear that "the natural man receiveth not the things of the Spirit of God; for they are foolishness unto him; neither can he know them, because they are spiritually discerned (or discerned by the Spirit)" (1 Cor. 2:14). This dictum is certainly true in respect to the things of the Spirit of God in connection with the conception of Jesus in the virgin's womb.

"Great is the mystery of godliness"—this latter half of the phrase compels as much attention as the first. How gifted by the Spirit Paul was in expressing truth in arrestive and fitting language! Among the *mysteries* mentioned in Scripture, the particular one with which the apostle deals in the portion before us must surely be the deepest of them all, and is "the mystic secret of our Faith." He refers to it in a previous verse (1 Tim. 3:9). It is profitable to compare the various interpretations given of Paul's statement, *Great is the mystery of godliness:*

"Beyond dispute, great is that mystic secret, as set forth in our confession-chant."

"Great beyond the question is the mystery of our religion."

"The mystery of godliness is great."

"This religion of ours is a tremendous mystery."

"The hidden truth of godliness is great."

It is necessary to possess a virgin life if the mystery of our Lord's virgin birth is to be rightly appreciated. By that we mean that one cannot fully understand the revealed facts of this holy mystery unless his life is made and kept holy by the same blessed Holy Ghost who carried through the wondrous conception of our Savior's human body.

In fact, one wonders if any particular part of our Lord's person and work can be rightly understood unless there is a corresponding spiritual experience. For instance, how can we grasp the tremendous miracle of our Lord's birth unless, first of all, we have been born again by the same Holy One who made Christ's birth possible?

Or how can we follow the Master's footsteps as He trod the streets of Galilee, and other parts, living a holy, sinless life amid the pollutions of earth, "the lily among thorns," unless we ourselves are seeking to live our lives unsullied by the ways and pursuits of this world?

Or how can we enter rightly into the sorrow of His rejection by His brethren, or the persecution by His friends and foes alike, or His tragic betrayal by a professed disciple, unless, in some measure, we have had to tread the same thorn-strewn road, and received many wounds without cause?

Or how can we linger under the shadow of Gethsemane's olive trees, and penetrate the meaning and mystery of His soul agony as He cries, "Not My will but Thine be done," unless we have come to some Gethsemane of surrender of our own, and learn to say, "The cup which my Father hath given me, shall I not drink it?"

Or how can we grasp the significance of His cross as He dies, unless we ourselves have come to the place of death, even to the place called

Calvary, that is "a skull," suggesting thereby nothingness, emptiness, and death?

Or how can we realize the truth of His glorious resurrection unless we are walking in the "newness of life"?

You see the thought! The apprehension of the truth concerning Christ requires a spiritual correspondence. Or, in other words, to know Christ, we must live Christ! And so we return to our opening word, namely, that the virgin birth of our Lord can only be profitably meditated upon by men and women whose lives are virgin.

Now, it is with the feeling of hesitation that one approaches this solemn, holy mystery of our Lord's entrance into our world as a human Babe. The theme is so vast and delicate, so profound and incomprehensible, that one trembles lest one word should be expressed that misrepresents in the least degree such a wonderful revelation.

May the same Holy Spirit who overshadowed Mary as she conceived her Son overshadow our hearts and minds as we seek to set forth the revealed truths regarding "the mystery of godliness: God manifest in the flesh"!

Mystery Versus Mist

Before we come to the main teaching of our subject, it may be fitting to clear the ground, so to speak. For although the virgin birth is in many respects a mystery, and will ever remain so, yet there is a good deal of so-called mystery which is nothing else but mist.

Mist

Now mist is not mystery. It can therefore be penetrated and cleared away! Often the mist of vague, partial, mistaken notions, of misunderstanding leading to half-truths, surround the fact of our Lord's virgin birth, thereby making the mystery itself needlessly greater.

And so, as one can rise above the natural mist by climbing the hill, or mountain, so by the aid of the Holy Spirit, our Divine Teacher and Revealer, we can rise above all the false or partial conceptions of this august truth we are considering, and comprehend simply and fully all that we ought to. The same Holy Spirit who conceived our Lord is perfectly willing to take of this matter that belongs to Christ, and shew it unto us!

Mystery

Of course, let no one imagine that he can explain or understand the mystery of the virgin birth, even after all the mist has been dispelled. No matter what light we may receive, the mystery of the God-Man in one Person remains.

Bishop Handley Moule asserts that "in Scripture a mystery may be a fact which, when revealed, we cannot understand in detail, though we can know it, and act upon it. . . . It is a thing only to be known when revealed." And in reference to the virgin birth, it is certainly true that "we cannot understand it in detail, though we can know it, and act upon it."

In the presence of such a holy miracle, "there can be no fitting attitude," to use the words of Dr. Morgan, "of the human intellect save that of acceptance of the truth, without any attempt to explain the absolute mystery."[3] Truly Paul was right when he declared that "without controversy great is the mystery of godliness," which mystery is "God manifest in the flesh" (1 Tim. 3:16). Yes, this mystery is great, too great even for our finite minds to comprehend! Mystery! Why, who can unravel this?

> The Ancient of Days begins as a Babe at Bethlehem!
> He who thunders in the heavens cries in a cradle!
> He who gives all their meat in due season, sucks the Breast!
> He who made all flesh is now made of flesh!
> The Mother is younger than the child she bears!
> He who could summon legions of angels is wrapped in
> swaddling clothes!
> The Mighty God is now a helpless infant!
> The Everlasting Father becomes a child!
> God and man become One Person!

No wonder an anonymous wise man has said, "I can scarce get past His cradle in my pausing to wonder at His cross. The infant Jesus is in

---

[3]G. Campbell Morgan, *The Crises of the Christ* (New York: Fleming H. Revell Co., 1903) 70.

some views a greater marvel than Jesus with the purple robe and the crown of thorns!"

Fathom the mystery! Never! We can only bow before it in holy wonder and marvel at the greatness of the God who could make such a wondrous birth as our Savior's possible. Let us take heed lest we rush in where angels fear to tread. Rather let our attitude be as the one depicted thus:

> I will seek to believe rather than to reason;
> to adore rather than to explain;
> to give thanks rather than to penetrate;
> to love rather than to know;
> to humble myself rather than to speak.

Faith Versus Reason

Reverently submitting to the presence of mystery in the fact of our Lord's virgin birth, we are led to consider another introductory thought, namely, that although the revealed truth of such a fact may be contrary to human reason, yet to the believer it is faith, and not reason, that must of necessity operate.

Many have stumbled over the question of the virgin birth simply because they have tried to explain it by human reasoning, but such a question baffles explanation. And so our position to all adverse criticism must be: "Well! here is a scriptural fact! We cannot fully understand it, but we accept and believe it!"

Reason would say, "Christ born of a virgin: Impossible!" And yet, Huxley, when appealed to, declared that as a scientific man he could not reject Christianity on the ground of the virgin birth, as there were millions of such births in the lower forms of life.

The virgin birth an impossibility! So may reason declare; but faith learns to accept the angel's word, even as Mary did when her reason failed to comprehend the truth, namely: "With God nothing shall be impossible" (Luke 1:37). Yes, and faith delights to respond, even as Mary did, ("Be it . . . according to thy word" (Luke 1:38).

> Seek not the cause, for 'tis not in thy reach,
> Of all the truths prophetic volumes teach,

Those "secret things" imparted from on high,
Which speak at once, and veil the Deity.
Pass on; nor rush to explore the depths that lie
Divinely hid in sacred mystery."

Now that we have traveled so far in seeking to prove the fact of the virgin birth, thereby confirming our faith, let us now go on to reverently handle the mystical truth that such a sacred theme presents. And in doing so let us remember our opening thought, that the mystery itself cannot be explained. With reverent, adoring hearts we accept and believe it.

1. The Miracle of the Mystery

The question from the most ancient book in the world is: "How can he be clean that is born of a woman?" (Job 25:4). The miracle of the virgin birth is that our Lord was absolutely clean, although He was born of a woman. The mystery of how such a miracle was effected we have already seen, but let us view the matter from another aspect. Look for a moment at the pedigree of Christ! In Matthew's genealogy, for instance, four women, Tamar (1:3), Ruth (1:5), Rahab (1:5) and Bathsheba (1:6), are mentioned as having been among the ancestors of our Lord. Three of them had been notoriously sinful, while the fourth, Ruth, was a Gentile alien. From an ancestry so tainted, it would have been impossible to have produced one who, like our Lord, possessed a sinless nature unless some miracle had taken place. And the miracle of the mystery of His birth is that in spite of the sinful pedigree He possessed, through the conception of the Holy Spirit He came into the world a perfectly sinless Person.

And in this there is an evidence of His peerless grace. He who was the highest stoops to the lowest; He who was so holy makes Himself of no reputation, but identifies Himself with sin-stained humanity that He might go down to the lowest steps of human need and debasement to raise fallen humanity up to purity and back to God.

2. The Mystery of the Miracle

Reversing the order of our words, let us reverently consider the stupendous mystery that reposes within the heart of the miracle of the virgin birth, like some precious jewel within a casket. There are, it would seem, two sides of the Mystery:

a. The combination of deity and humanity.

It is a great wonder indeed to realize that the Holy Spirit framed the body of Christ within the virgin's body, but the wonder and mystery are intensified when we remember that the Holy Spirit united deity and humanity together. God and man were combined by the Holy Spirit and formed into One Person. This is a great mystery, baffling explanation, and one which the angels pry into with adoration.

Dr. Handley Moule remarks that "God did not send His Son to join a man born of a woman; which would have been an alliance of two persons, not a harmony of two natures in relation to one person." Oh, beloved, how incomprehensible is the mystery! Through the Holy Ghost our Lord became not God and Man, but "the God-Man." He was truly "God manifest in the flesh"! That man should be made in God's image was a wonder, but that God should be made in man's image is a greater wonder.

In his despair Job cried, "Neither is there any daysman betwixt us, that might lay his hand upon us both" (9:33). But Christ is our Daysman: "The God-man!" says Dr. Pierson. "The daysman betwixt us both, who can lay his hand upon us both, because He is of us both! The way of God to man—the way of man to God; the true Jacob's ladder between heaven and earth, God above it, to come down—man beneath it, to go up! The God-man is Himself our pledge that as God in Christ became a partaker of the human nature, so man in Christ becomes a partaker of the divine nature. Born of a woman, made like unto Him! The God-man is not only a mystery and a miracle, but a prophecy and a promise . . . They used to say of Mozart that he brought angels down; of Beethoven, that he lifted mortals up. Jesus Christ does both, and here lies the central mystery of the God-man, a mystery which is blessedly revealed to him who by faith has personal experience of His power to save."

And so one side of the mystery of the miracle is that "at the birth of Jesus of Nazareth there came into existence one Personality, such as, with reference to the duality of its nature, had never had existence before," as Dr. Morgan puts it.[4]

---

[4] Morgan, *Crises*, 82–83.

b. Pre-existent, yet born a child.

We now come to a phase of our holy meditation that fills our hearts with adoring wonder, namely, why and how Christ was begotten apart from the ordinary course of nature.

If Christ had come from human parents, such would have meant that He was not existent before His human birth, but that His beginning commenced with His birth. Every child born into the world marks the beginning of a new life, a life that has not existed before. Now Christ was the Pre-existent One which is seen (apart from all other scriptural evidence such as John 1:1) in Luke 1:35. Following the marginal reading of the Revised Version we read (and carefully observe the language), "The Holy Thing which is to be born shall be called the Son of God." Such implies that while some are holy after their birth, Christ was holy before it. "The Holy Thing *which is*."

And so the virgin birth, because it was not a birth according to natural generation, that is, as the result of the sacred relationship of human parents to each other, did not create Christ. It only gave Him who existed from all eternity a human body in which to come and die for all mankind. And as one can easily see, nothing but a "virgin birth" could produce such a Preexistent One.

3. The Message of the Miracle and Mystery

Why was it that our Lord condescended to limit Himself in this fashion? Why did He, the Preexistent One, take upon Himself the likeness of sinful flesh and commence from the same starting place as ourselves? The answer is that the virgin birth was essential to the redemption and regeneration of humanity. In an excellent way this is described by Dr. Morgan: "Man's ruin was so terrible and so profound, as witness the darkened intelligence, the deadened emotion, and the degraded will, that there was but one alternative open to the Eternal God. Either He must sweep out and destroy utterly the race, or else in infinite patience and through long processes, lead it back to Himself. He chose the pathway of reconciliation in His infinite grace, at what cost the story of the Christ alone perfectly reveals . . . The God-man then is the gateway between God and man. Through Him God has found His way back to man, from whom He had been excluded by his rebellion. In Him man finds his way back to God from whom he had been alienated by the darkening of his intelligence, the death of his love, and the disobedience of his will."[5]

Or we can give the message of our Lord's virgin birth in the following summary that is enlarged upon in Watson's "Body of Divinity."

> The *causa prima*, and impulsive cause, was free grace. Not our deserts but our misery made Christ take flesh . . . Christ incarnate is nothing but love covered with flesh.
>
> Christ took our flesh upon Him, that He might take our sins upon Him. He was the greatest sinner, having the weight of the sins of the whole world lying upon Him.
>
> Christ took our flesh that He might make the human nature appear lovely to God, and the divine nature appear lovely to man.
>
> Jesus Christ united Himself to man, that man might be drawn nearer to God.
>
> He was poor, that He might make us rich.
> He was born of a virgin, that we might be born of God.
> He took our flesh, that He might give us the Spirit.
> He lay in the manger that we might lie in Paradise.
> He came down from heaven, that He might bring us to heaven.

And what was all this but love? If our hearts be not rocks, this love of Christ should affect us. Behold love that passeth knowledge! Such then is the message of our Lord's virgin birth.

---

[5] Ibid., 88, 90.

2

HIS INCARNATION

The Word was made flesh (John 1:14)
God was manifest in the flesh (1 Tim. 3:16)

Christ as Incarnate

The commanding line in the "confession-chant" which Paul quotes is made up of only six words, but what a world of tremendous truth is condensed in them: "*God was manifest in the flesh*"! Is this not a conspicuous illustration of the proverb *Multum in parvo*—much in small compass? Because the virgin birth of our Lord is "*the* pillar and main-stay of the truth," we must devote as much space to such a foundational tenet of our Christian faith as possible.

It may help to clear away some of the unnecessary mist that has gathered around this sublime, sacred mystery of the virgin birth of our Lord, if we give a somewhat brief consideration to the terms, scriptural and otherwise, that are used to denote it.

The Immaculate Conception

This term is often incorrectly applied to the virgin birth, thus committing a manifest blunder, seeing it confuses one idea with another.

A Papal Bull called "*Ineffabilis Deus*" brought into force the above term. This particular Papal Bull was promulgated by Pope Pius IX on December 8, 1854. In this Catholic dogma the central proclamation is that, "from the first moment of her conception [that is, her own conception] the Blessed Virgin Mary was, by the singular grace and privilege of Almighty God, and in view of the merits of Jesus Christ, the Saviour of Mankind, kept free from all stain of Original Sin." Such a new doctrine was enforced to glorify Mary, the Mother of God, as the Catholic Church calls her, and give her a more exalted place by lifting her out of the realm of human beings, and endow her with divine attributes and functions.

Therefore "the Immaculate Conception" does not refer to our Lord's birth, but to the supposed sinlessness of Mary from the moment when she was conceived within her own mother's womb.

The Incarnation

Although this is not a scriptural word, yet it is one we often employ in connection with the virgin birth of our Lord. The word "incarnate" means "to embody in flesh." And this is what really happened to Mary's Child. "The Word became flesh!" or "God was manifested or embodied in flesh"!

"Veiled in flesh the God-head see!
Hail the Incarnate Deity!"

But "Incarnation" is a broad word and is identified not only with our Lord's entrance into our world as a Babe, but with His whole life from that moment on. Throughout the days of His flesh He was the Incarnate One; and He still is, for in glory He possesses the human form that He died and rose with, although glorified. He is still "this same Jesus"! And the wonder in heaven now, and forever, is the presence of Him who is "the God-Man."

The Supernatural or Miraculous Birth

This designation, although often quoted, will not even do unless we fully understand what we mean when we use it. The birth of our Lord itself was not supernatural or miraculous. By this we mean that there is no intimation that the process of birth was in any way exceptional. Perfectly natural phenomena are suggested by the Messianic utterance of Psalm 22:9–10 (which see). Mary's Child was formed within her womb, and then born in just the same natural way as was the child of Elizabeth, Mary's cousin.

The miraculous element was not in the formation of our Lord's body, but in the manner of its begetting. The birth of our Lord is only supernatural in that He was virgin born, that is, apart from the ordinary course of nature. It is in this sense that we can view both Mary's and Elizabeth's conception as miraculous.

The birth of our Lord was miraculous in that Mary bore Him as a result of a divine creative act, apart from human generation. The birth of John the Baptist was also miraculous in that Elizabeth, his mother, had traveled beyond the age when through the ordinary course of nature it was possible for a woman to conceive and bear.

Or to quote A.T. Schofield: "Both births, therefore, were supernatural; that to Elizabeth was because it was *too late*, that to Mary because it was *too soon*."

The Virgin Birth

With Dr. Sweet we agree that the only statement which is sufficiently specific is "virgin birth," inasmuch as according to the New Testament statement Mary was at the time of this birth *virgo intacto*. But not only is "the virgin birth" a title "sufficiently specific," it is the only scriptural way of describing such, and is therefore the most correct term.

1. Born of a Virgin

There are two passages that supply the fact of our Lord's virgin birth.

The Prediction of It. "Behold, a virgin shall conceive, and bear a son, and shall call His name Immanuel" (Isa. 7:14).

The Fulfillment of It. "Now, all this was done (that is, the work of the Holy Ghost in 1:20, 21), that it might be fulfilled which was spoken of the Lord by the prophet, saying, Behold, a virgin shall be with child, and shall bring forth a son, and they shall call his name Immanuel" (Matt. 1:22, 23).

Arising out of these statements are one or two questions that demand our study and attention:

a. What is a virgin?

The term "virgin" appears to have a twofold application, at least when used in reference to a woman. There is the world "Almah" which denotes any young unmarried woman, whether she has kept her virginity, that is, preserved the purity of her body, or otherwise. Then there is the other word "Parthenos," which signifies a young unmarried woman who has preserved the purity of her body; one who is a "*virgo intacto.*"

The former is the word that we have in the Hebrew of Isaiah 7:14, while the latter word is the one that the *LXX* translators have given us, because to them it conveyed the significance mentioned. And it is the latter word that the angel reiterates in his message to Joseph in Matthew 1:23.

So the logical conclusion is that Mary as a Virgin was a "young unmarried woman who had preserved the purity of her body," to use Cruden's phrase again. And not only so, but that Mary remained a virgin until after Christ was born is the revealed fact of Scripture, as anyone can prove by reverently examining passages like Matthew 1:18–21; 1:24–25; Luke 1:27–34. Thereafter she lived in the usual relations of wedlock with Joseph, having children born unto her (Matt. 13:55, 56).

b. Why was Christ born of a virgin?

This second question is not so easily answered as the first. One very old writer suggests three reasons:

"For Decency"

It became not God to have any mother but a maid, and it became not a maid to have any other son but God.

"For Necessity"

If our Lord had been born according to the laws of natural procreation He would have been defiled. Had He had a human father, as well as a human mother, then with the Psalmist He would have had to cry, "Behold, I was shapen in iniquity; and in sin did my mother conceive me!" (Ps. 51:5).

All who are born after the ordinary course of nature have the tincture of sin within. But Christ is to be absolutely sinless: "holy, harmless, undefiled, separated from sinners." His substance must be pure and immaculate; otherwise, His right to redeem is forfeited. Hence He must be virgin born! In the formation of His body there must be no original sin, so that He can commence where Adam did; thus in Him there was not the mixture of human seed. Well we might say:

> Approach, thou gentle Little One,
> Of stainless Mother born to earth,
> Free from all wedded union
> The Mediator's twofold birth.
> What joys to the vast universe
> In that chaste Maiden's womb are borne;
> Ages set free from sorrow's curse
> Spring forth, the everlasting morn.

Melchizedec was a type of Christ, who is said to be "without father and mother." Christ being born of a virgin answered the type; He was without father and mother; without mother He was as God; without father He was as Man.

c. How could Christ be born of a virgin, and yet be without sin?

Doubtless this question has troubled some minds. Christ we declare was made of the flesh and blood of a virgin, and as the purest virgin is stained with original sin, how could our Lord be without sin? "How can he be clean that is born of a woman" (Job 25:4)?

This seemingly difficult knot is untied for us in Luke 1:35. "The Holy Ghost shall come upon thee, and the power of the Highest shall overshadow thee; therefore also that holy thing (human body of Christ) which shall be born of thee shall be called the Son of God."

Mark the phrase, "The Holy Ghost shall overshadow thee," for it means that the Holy Spirit consecrated and purified that part of the virgin's flesh whereof Christ was made. "As the alchemist extracts and draws away the dross from the gold, so the Holy Ghost refines and clarifies that part of the virgin's flesh, separating it from sin. Though the Virgin Mary herself had sin, yet that part of her flesh whereof Christ was made was without sin, otherwise it must have been an impure conception."

2. Born of the Holy Ghost

The angel of the Lord in banishing the doubts of Joseph regarding Mary's purity and morality announces: "For that which is conceived in her is of the Holy Ghost" (Matt. 1:20).

This term gives us the birth of our Lord from its divine side, just as the following one gives us the birth from the human side. Professor Orr remarks: "There is another factor—'conceived by the Holy Ghost.' What happened was a divine, created miracle wrought in the production of this new humanity which secured from its earliest germinal beginnings freedom from the slightest taint of sin."

3. Born of a Woman

In Galatians 4:4 Paul declares that "when the fullness of the time was come, God set forth his Son, made of a woman, made under the law." Such a phrase describes the perfect humanity of our Lord and gives us His wondrous birth from the human standpoint. But one may ask the question: Why was Christ born of a woman? Well, there are one or two answers to such a question:

4. As a Fulfillment of Promise

The great redemption promise of Genesis 3:15 was: "It (the seed of the woman) shall bruise thy (the serpent's) head." Woman who was made a sinner by the serpent will produce One who will destroy the serpent's power. And so in 1 Timothy 2:15, "She shall be saved through her (or the) child-bearing" (R.V.), some scholars find an allusion to the promise of Genesis 3:15. Evident it is that woman is saved from her sin through the Child born of the woman, even Mary, who is highly favored among women.

5. As a Removal of Reproach

By being "born of a woman" Christ has rolled away the reproach from woman which became hers by the seduction of the serpent. In taking her flesh our Lord honors her sex and thereby unties the knot of Eve's disobedience. The writers of the early church, we are told, often pressed this analogy between Eve and Mary in language similar to this: "As at the first the woman had made man a sinner, so now, to make him amends, she brings him a Saviour."

Two other terms: Born a king (Matt. 2:2)

and

Born a Savior (Luke 2:111)

each express different truths.

The following outline might be of use for a "Christmas" sermon. The virgin birth of our Lord was a

1. Predicted Birth (Isa. 9:6; Micah 5:2; Matt. 2:5, 6).

2. Miraculous Birth (Matt. 1:18–20; Luke 1:35). Creative act of God, not of man. Notice phraseology.

3. Virgin Birth (Matt. 1:16, 23, 25; Luke 2:7; Col. 1:15–18; Heb. 12:23; 1:5, 6; John 3:16).

4. Holy Birth (Luke 1:35; John 9:34; Ps. 51:5; 58:3; See Job 15:14; 25:4).

5. Lowly Birth (Luke 2:7, 12–16; Gal. 4:4).

6. Royal Birth (Matt. 2:2, 6; Luke 2:11; John 18:37).

7. Beneficial Birth (Matt. 1:21; Gal. 4:4, 5; 1 Tim. 1:15; Prov. 17:17).

Christ's Form as God

When God created man with a perfect human body, and inspired the historian to record, "God created man, in the likeness of God made he him," the same does not imply that God has a physical frame such as He fashioned for Adam (Gen. 1:26, 27; 5:1). While God uses bodily organs, such as eyes, ears, mouth, hands, and feet, in describing His provision and purposes for His children, the same are used in a symbolic sense. Having formed the eye, "shall he not see?" (Ps. 94:9). As "no man hath seen God at any time," we do not know what form, in His person, He possesses. Certainly His divine essence veiled in human form was seen (Gen. 18:2; 32:30).

Before his incarnation, as the only begotten Son of God, Jesus shared the same ethereal form as His Father, but at His birth, God became especially incarnate in His Son, so much so, that He could say, "He that hath seen me, hath seen the Father" (John 14:9). But this does not mean that God had a human body, such as Jesus assumed. The likeness of God in Adam, and also that of Jesus to God, represent the possession of the same spiritual and moral qualities of God (John 14:7–12). Jesus said, "I and my father are one" (John 10:30). All that God is, and was willing to do for man, Jesus came to be and do. In God, we find tender love, melting compassion, and gracious forbearance; mercy and power, rectitude and pity, holiness and long suffering, justice and harmlessness, united. And, both the Father and the Son were one in these virtues. This is why we should always look at God in Christ, and not from any other angle, even nature.

Did not Jesus declare, "I have manifested thy name" (John 17:6)? This does not infer the mere repetition of a particular name but the nature, being of God—all God is in Himself. What He is, that Jesus manifested to those about Him. This is why He received the name *Immanuel*, which means, "God with us." As S.D. Gordon appealingly expresses it:

> Jesus was the mind of God, thinking out to man—
> the heart of God throbbing love out to man's heart—
> the face of God looking into man's face—
> the voice of God speaking into man's ears—
> the hand of God, strong and tender, reaching down to take man by the hand.

> Till God in human flesh I see,
> My thoughts no comfort find:

The holy, just, and sacred *Three,*
Are terrors to my mind:
But if Immanuel's face appear,
My soul surmounts each slavish fear.

In one of the most marvelous yet mysterious sections of the Bible we have the record of a man who saw more of God than any other person in history. God said that He knew this privileged man by name. Already Moses had received assurance from God who spoke to him face to face, as a man speaking with his friend, that Divine presence and protection would be his as he continued to lead Israel to the promised land (Exod. 23:20–25). But the deep, spiritual nature of Moses craved for something greater, and so he requested, "I beseech thee, shew me thy glory" (Exod. 33:18). All that he had seen of God was insufficient, thus he sought for that beatific vision granted as the final reward of them perfected in another world.

God, however, could not grant all Moses desired, for no mortal man could possibly behold the full glory of God and live. He is "the king . . . invisible" (1 Tim. 1:17) and "whom no man hath seen, nor can see" (6:16). What God allowed was "all His goodness to pass before Moses," and Moses also to witness an actual portion of His glory; Moses saw as much as any man could gaze upon, and more, probably, than any other saint will ever witness until in God's actual presence above. It is to be understood that when God spoke of His face, hands and back parts, the same were used figuratively in the wonderful climax of the blessed interview between God and His friend. As God's *glory* passed by Moses saw the hinder part of it, that is, the afterglow of such an effulgence. Ellicott's *Commentary* fittingly summarizes the concluding verses of this remarkable episode thus:

> Human nature is, by its very nature, unfit for expression of sublime spiritual truths, and necessarily clothes them in a materialistic garment which is alien to their ethereal nature. All that we can legitimately gather from these verses 22 and 23 is that Moses was directed to a certain retired position, where God miraculously both protected him and shrouded him, while a manifestation of His glory passed by of a transcendent character, and that Moses was allowed to see, not the full manifestation, but the sort of

afterglow which is left behind, which was as much as human nature could endure.

Yet the inescapable truth is that in Jesus His disciples could gaze upon the glory of God and live. "We beheld his glory, the glory as of the only begotten of the Father"—the original form of God Jesus possessed (John 1:14). Paul spoke of Jesus as "the *image* of the invisible God" (Col. 1:15). As the *word*, Jesus was the image of the invisible thought of God. Then in the initial miracle of His public ministry, Jesus turned the water into wine and "*manifested forth his glory*" thereby (John 2:11). What happened at the wedding feast in Cana of Galilee was the first sign, signally the manifestation of the sum of divine attributes, now shining forth to the eyes and hearts of men. This miracle of love was not performed simply to appeal to the imagination—none of the miracles of Jesus were mere wonders, but visible emblems of all He was, of all that He came to do as the only begotten Son of the Father. His miracles were "radiant images of the permanent miracle of the manifestation of Christ."

To the inner significance of this first public manifestation of His glory, John appends the profound effect upon His own, "and his disciples believed in him" (John 2:11). Seeing Him invested with all power and glory as the Messiah, they rested their faith in Him. And so, to quote Godet:

> These glorious irradiations from the person of Jesus, which are called miracles, are, therefore, designed not only, as apologetics often assume, to strike the eyes of the still unbelieving multitude and to stimulate the delaying, but, especially, to illuminate the hearts of believers, by revealing to them, in this world of suffering, all the riches of the living Object of their faith.[1]

Further, in the Transfiguration of Jesus, we have the most striking evidence that He came as "God manifest in the flesh." Peter, James and John were smitten with partial blindness, as the brilliant glory of God outflashed in the altered countenance of Jesus, and His raiment "be-

---

[1] Frederick Louis Godet, *Commentary on the Gospel of John* (Grand Rapids: Zondervan Publishing House; reprint from 3d French edition, 1893), 352.

came shining, exceeding white as snow, so as no fuller on earth could white them" (Mark 9:3). Dazzled and afraid of such a manifestation of glory, not only in Jesus, but in the glorified bodies of Moses and Elijah, the disciples found themselves enveloped by a cloud, and in it heard God with assuring voice say, "This is my beloved Son: hear him" (Mark 9:7). That trio of privileged disciples saw God's glory reflected in their Master, *and they lived.*

Once they were able to open their half-blinded eyes again, "they saw no man . . . save Jesus only" (Mark 9:8). The glorified heavenly visitants had vanished, as did the outflashing of their Master's inherent glory. Again, He was *Jesus,* with His accustomed form they dearly loved. Now, in this age of salvation, no man can truly live unless he sees Jesus as the embodiment of both the glory and the grace of God. When He became flesh and dwelt among men, Jesus humanized deity, and deified humanity.

Jesus Himself affirmed that *God is Spirit* and that a *Spirit* does not possess "flesh and blood," such as He assumed in His incarnation. His disciples were affrighted that He was some kind of ghost or phantom form, so He invited them to handle Him, and to test the reality of His pierced hands and side. How consoled they were as they heard Him say, "It is I myself" (Luke 24:39), and saw the evident proofs of corporeal resurrection. As they watched Him eat, they realized that Jesus was still in the body in which He had lived for more than thirty-three years, withal now glorified and spiritual, but manifested under sensible conditions to prove that it was the same body which was nailed to a tree (John 20:24–28; Luke 24).

"Flesh and bones" represent the solid and tangible framework of the body. "Blood" is not mentioned, yet the term "flesh" implies it (1 Cor. 15:50). The blood is the life of the animal and corruptible body, which cannot inherit the kingdom of God (Gen. 9:4; 1 Cor. 15:50). "Flesh and bones," then, imply the identity, but with diversity of laws, of the resurrection body, in which, in some mysterious way, Jesus could pass through closed doors. What form God the Father, and God the Spirit, have eternally possessed is one of the unanswered questions our entrance into their presence will alone reveal. Meantime, we rest by faith in the statement of Jesus Himself that, "He that hath seen me, hath seen the Father" (John 14:9).

What must be made clear is the fact that as the Word, or *Logos*, Jesus did not lay aside the essence of God, but only the form, whatever that is like. He did not pass from the divine state into that of a mere man, but entered into our nature, taking upon Himself the likeness of man. He was not merely assuming such likeness, but He *became flesh*. Thus, the grand doctrine of John's Gospel is that Jesus, as the Divine Revealer of God entering our humanity, thereby becomes one with us. The two leading ideas of John in this connection are *testimony* and *faith*, the former to the end of the latter (10:30–42). "Only the Highest could make Himself the lowest," and this is what Jesus accomplished by the union of His eternal divine nature with a human nature. In His incarnation He became what He was not before—*flesh*.

The eternal, uncreated Word, who in His divine nature was with God in eternity, and was equal with God, did not join Himself to some human being, but became *Man*. Whoever met Him in the days of His flesh met God's Son in human dress. Perfect deity and perfect humanity were His, and as Godet says, "The content of John's declaration (of the Word becoming flesh does not mean) two natures or two opposite modes of being co-existing in the same subject; but a single subject passing from one mode of being to another, in order to recover the first by perfectly realizing the second."[2] When, at His Ascension, He recovered His divine station and state, He did not renounce His human personality but exalted it even to the point where it is the organ of His divine state. Jesus ever remains, "The man, Christ Jesus."

True faith recognizes in Jesus, the only begotten Son coming from the presence of His Father—the *Being* God-*given*, and God-*revealed* in a human existence. This, beyond any shadow of doubt, is the foundational truth of the New Testament, and it is recorded for our inspiration and comfort. On earth, and now in heaven, He is the One ever touched with the feeling of our infirmities, seeing He was tested and tried as we are, and added lustre to His perfection through suffering.

O Saviour Christ, Thou too art Man;
Thou has been troubled, tempted, tried;

---

[2] Ibid., 270.

Thy kind but searching glance can scan
The very wounds that shame would hide.

Being found in fashion as a man involved for Jesus being tempted as a man, thus He was tempted in all points as man has ever been, yet different from man in that He never yielded to any temptation. In this, He was separate from the sinners He came to save. He could confess, "I do always these things that please him (my Father)" (John 8:29). It is the testimony of Scripture that while on earth He, as the Son of Man, "learned . . . obedience by the things which he suffered" (Heb. 5:8). Another important fact to remember is that Jesus not only claimed prerogatives of deity, and exercised them to prove that He was the God-Man, but although He was active throughout His public ministry performing miracles for the physical and mental benefit of the afflicted, He never used such prerogatives to relieve or satisfy any human need of His own. When we read, "he *suffered* being tempted" (Heb. 2:18), the implication is that He drank any bitter cup the Father permitted to its dregs. "The cup which my Father hath given me, shall I not drink it" (John 18:11)?

Christ's Temptation as Man

A forcible illustration of this self-imposed limitation in some of the crises of Christ can be found in His *Temptation*, from which as "the man Christ Jesus," He emerged victorious. In passing, it is interesting to observe that some of the language Paul used in his epitome of the Incarnation in 1 Timothy 3:16, can be traced in the Temptation record. Christ came as God manifest in flesh, "The Word was God" and twice over He reminded Satan that He was "The Lord thy God" (Matt. 4:8), although visible to the tempter in human form. Paul also said that Christ was justified by the Spirit, and Matthew tells us that the self-same Spirit masterminded the Temptation. Then, when the conflict was over there is the association of angels with Christ as they came to minister unto Him (Matt. 4:1–11).

But now, let us look more closely at Satan's threefold attempt to persuade Christ to use His miraculous power as God, not only to prove that He was God, but also to alleviate His own physical needs as

Man—needs He had miraculously supplied for other humans, as Matthew goes on to record (4:23, 24. See Luke 3:21, 22; 4:1–13). We cannot approach the absorbing experience as given by Matthew and Luke, without being deeply impressed by the marked contrast of the two connected days in connection with the Temptation of our Lord.

On the day of His water baptism by John, there came the further baptism with the Holy Spirit, with the heavens opening and shedding their radiance upon Him who had come to dwell among men, with the acknowledgment by God that He was His own beloved Son. What a glorious day! But the next day—what a drastic change, with its hunger, peril, and darkness. Yet it was the heavenly baptism of the one day that prepared Jesus for the hellish battle of the next day. After the Dove, there came the Devil, but the Dove prevailed.

One cannot consider the unique verse introducing the Temptation record without recalling the quotation from Bishop Hall's *Contemplations* which Thomas Timpson cites in his remarkable volume on *The Angels of God* (perhaps the most valuable and voluminous study of angelic ministry ever written). It was published in 1845 and is now almost impossible to obtain. Exclaimed the godly Bishop:

> O the depth of the wisdom of God! How camest Thou, O Saviour, to be thus tempted? That Spirit whereby Thou wast conceived as man, and which was one with Thee and the Father as God, led Thee into the wilderness to be tempted of Satan!—And why did it please Thee, O Saviour, to fast forty days and forty nights, unless, as Moses fasted forty days at the *delivery* of the Law, and Elijah at the restitution of the Law, so thou thoughtest fit, at the *accomplishment* of the law and the promulgation of the gospel, to fulfil the time of both of these types of Thine."[3]

Full of the Holy Spirit, Jesus came to a desert place, that in its solitude, "He might vent to those sacred passions, which the late grand occurrences of the descent of the Spirit upon Him, and the miraculous

---

[3]Thomas Timpson, *The Angels of God* (London: Paternoster Row, 1845) 403–4.

attestation of a voice from Heaven, had such a tendency to inspire," as Doddridge expresses it in his study on *Luke.*

Having received His inauguration or consecration to His office, as well as His Father's attestation at Jordan, Jesus received the endowment for His three years of public ministry through the baptism with the Holy Spirit, and His Spirit-led temptation should not be approached apart from such a baptism, which fortified Him against His conflict with Satan. Thirty years was a long time to wait for such a brief period of service, but what momentous events were crowded into such a period. Those three years of service among men changed the world.

Only seventeen words, but what contrasts they contain! "Then (when? After Matt. 3:13–17) was *Jesus* led up of the *Spirit* into the wilderness (contrast to Jordan) to be tempted of the devil" (Matt. 4:1). Led of the Spirit—tempted of the devil! The more one lives under the sway of the Spirit, the fiercer the assault of Satan. Because no other has ever been so possessed by the Spirit, as Jesus the God-Man was, no other has ever experienced the full anger of hell as He did. The holier the life, the fiercer the onslaught of the unholy tempter, who hates above everything else when the believer is victorious over his snares, and the consequent perfecting of holiness in the hearts of those he tempts.

Led

How arrestive is this past participle of *lead*, meaning to guide! Paul would have us remember that, "As many as are *led* by the Spirit of God, they are the sons of God" (Rom. 8:14). Jesus, who became the Son of man, revealed Himself as the Son of God, when, in unison with the Spirit of God, He went into the wilderness to be tempted of the devil. Coming as the Lamb, slain before the foundations of the world, He knew that His would be constant encounters with the devil, until He destroyed his power, so He was not led by the Spirit against His will, but willingly acquiesced in the Spirit's guidance.

At the beginning of His ministry Jesus was led by the Spirit to be tempted of the devil, and at the end of His public career, devil-inspired men led Him out as a Lamb to the slaughter. For ourselves, it is well to yield, at each step of life, to the divine movings, even when they lead us somewhat mysteriously. The Spirit still leads into temptation, for when no self-invited, and rightly met, testing serves our best interests. It reveals our weaknesses, rouses our watchfulness, drives us to God for help, clears our aims and principles, and strengthens the soul in conflict. It is in this way the machinations of the devil are overruled for our spiritual good. Isaiah gives us a most appealing symbol of the Lord's power to use the devil in this way when he tells us that the Lord shaves "with a razor that is hired" (7:20). Says Richard Glover, "The Devil is the string of the kite—a downward pull, by resisting which we rise."[4]

Tempted

A comparison of the two most prominent temptations in Scripture is most instructive. The first temptation which came in Eden was yielded to, and so began the tragic history of sin in the world, resulting in death; this necessitated the second temptation in the wilderness, which was victoriously resisted and ultimately provided deliverance from sin and death for all who are tempted and defeated by the devil. So both Testaments begin with a record of satanic activity. The First Adam was tempted somewhat lightly in a beautiful garden, or in a universe yet unspoiled by sin. Hunger was not Adam's susceptibility to temptation, for all the perfect fruits of the garden surrounded him. But the Last Adam (1 Co. 15:45) was tempted when hungry in a wilderness, and yet successfully exhausted all the arts and darts of the wicked one. The temptation of Jesus occurred in "a world rendered desolate by Adam's Fall, and the ultimate effect of His victory will be to make it a Garden again . . . The one is the story of *Paradise Lost*; the other of the beginning of *Paradise Regained*."[5]

Leading and testing form a good combination for character building. If we are "led by the Spirit," we need not fear where the foundation is not touched. The oak has no fear of the tempest if its roots are firm. The First Adam had innocence but fell—revealing liability for disobedience to the will and Word of God, but not tendency. The Last Adam was sinless and thus had neither liability nor tendency. If He could

---

[4]Richard Glover, *A Teacher's Commentary on the Gospel of Matthew* (Grand Rapids: Zondervan Publishing House, 1956) 28.
[5]Ibid.

have sinned, then He could not have been our Redeemer. If He could not have been tempted, He could not have been one with us. As for ourselves we have both liability and tendency to yield to temptation because of inherited and inbred sin, and therefore we have more need to watch and pray that we enter not into temptation to be defeated.

> Yield not to temptation, for yielding is sin,
> Each victory will help you some other to win;
> Fight manfully onward, dark passions subdue,
> Look ever to Jesus, He'll carry you through.

The Devil

Three distinct designations are given this arch enemy from hell: *Devil, Tempter,* and *Satan* (Matt. 4:1, 3, 10). How convincingly these names prove the personality and power of the persistent adversary of Jesus. Though unseen, he is yet real and ever full of malignity even when he appears as an angel of light (2 Cor. 11:14). The devil of the Bible is repulsive: a creature with a horned head, cloven hoof and tail, as traditionally represented. As such he would be too hideous and obvious to deceive anyone.

This fearful being is apparently one of the cherubim God created to serve Him, being anointed for a position of great authority possibly over the primitive creation. But he fell through his pride and ambition, and was expelled from heaven. Ever since he has been the tireless enemy of both God and man (Isa. 14:12–14; Ezek. 28:11–15). The word *devil* is from "diabolus" meaning "to throw over" or "cast down," and true to this foul name he tempted Jesus to cast Himself down from the pinnacle of the temple. His name is also related to his own revolution and rejection, seeing he was cast out of heaven, and made the earth and the air the scene and seat of his unceasing diabolical activity (Luke 10:18; Eph. 2:2; 1 Pet. 5:8).

As for Jesus, the devil could not throw Him down. Now blessedly secure in the heavenlies, He is able to lift up the needy out of the devil's dunghill (Ps. 113:7; 147:6). At Calvary, the tempter was still *diabolus,* for the taunt of those he held captive was, "Let him now *come down* from the cross, and we will believe him" (Matt. 27:42). It is only faith that Jesus willingly stayed on His cross of shame and suffering for our sins that avails. "I, if I be lifted up from the earth, will draw all men unto me" (John 12:32).

Tempter

Such a dreaded name belongs to men, as well as to the devil and demons. Matthew names the heartless foe of God and men as *the tempter*, seeing he is the chief malignant enticer, who untiringly labors for the destruction of men. He is "weak in that he can only harm us by making us harm ourselves, but strong in his power of persuading us to do so"—a persuasion that had no influence whatever over the tempted Christ. As a tempter, he subtly chose a fitting time for his assault, namely, immediately after Christ's baptism, indicating that consecration to God incites temptation with all the arts of hell to slay such a dedication to God.

Then the devil also knew that in His hungry condition after such a long fast, Christ would be weak and physically unfit to resist the temptation to miraculously appease His hunger. As God, He could not be tempted with evil (James 1:13); therefore He met the tempter and conquered Him in the strength of His human nature, weak though He was, assisted by the enabling power of the Spirit. We might well wonder what it was that animated and emboldened the tempter to assail Christ as he did. Perhaps he thought that he would obtain as easy a victory over this Last Adam as he did over the First Adam in Paradise. Further, with the remembrance of his own fall, he might have arrogantly concluded that no heart, even the one that was "meek and lowly," could resist the temptation of pride and ambition. But how deluded the tempter was! Bennett in his *Lectures on the History of Christ*, asks the question:

> Could he, who afterwards proclaimed Christ to be the Son of the Most High God, and had perhaps but lately heard Him owned by such a voice from Heaven, make any doubt of His Divinity? Or, if he actually believed it, could he expect to vanquish him? We may conclude that he did not expect it; but mad with rage and despair, he was determined at least to worry that Lamb of God, which he knew he could not devour; and to vex with his hellish suggestions that innocent and holy soul, which he knew he could never seduce.

Many sincere Christians have been somewhat perplexed over the seeming contradiction between Jesus being led into temptation, and the petition in the prayer He taught His disciples to pray, "*Lead us not into temptation.*" This cannot mean freedom from conflict with the tempter, otherwise the phrase, "tempted as we are," would not be true of Him. What must be made clear is the fact that as Man, Christ acquired experimental ability to "succour them that are tempted" (Heb. 2:18). Ellicott's *Commentary* at Matthew 6:13 seems to have a satisfactory answer to this apparent prohibition regarding the saint being tempted, by pointing out that the Greek word for *temptation* includes two thoughts represented in English by *trials*, namely:

1. Sufferings which test or try.

2. Temptations, or allurements on this side of pleasure which tend to lead us into evil.

Of these the former is the dominant meaning in the language of the New Testament, and that is of which we must think here. See Matt. 26:41. We are taught not to think of the temptation in which lust meets opportunity as that into which God leads us, James 1:13, 14; there is therefore something which shocks us in the thought of asking Him not to lead us into it.

But the trials of another kind, persecution, spiritual conflicts, agony of body or of spirit, these may come to us as a test or as a discipline. Should we shrink from these? An ideal stoicism, a perfect faith, would say, "No, let us accept these and leave the issue in our Father's hands." But those who are conscious of their weakness cannot shake off that they might fail in the conflict, and the cry of that conscious weakness is therefore, "Lead us not into such trials," even as our Lord prayed, "If it be possible, let this cup pass away from Me" (Matt. 26:39).

The answer to the prayer may come either directly in actual exemption from the trial, or in "the way of escape" (1 Cor. 10:13), or in strength to bear it. It is hardly possible to read the prayer without thinking of the recent experience of *temptation* through which our Lord has passed. The memory of that trial in all its terrible aspects was still present with Him, and in His tender love for His disciples He bade them pray that they may not be led into anything so awful.

The two phrases, "Lead us not into temptation" and "Deliver us from evil" (or the evil one), can be made to imply that we seek deliverance from the sinister evil lurking in any temptation of the devil.

Satan

With the utterance of this most dreaded yet revealing name, Jesus plucked the mask from the enemy, who had assumed the fairest form to do his foulest deed, and flung it away, and left the naked wretch a miserable, convicted fiend. "Get thee hence *Satan.*" With the third temptation the resistance of Jesus was roused to the utmost pitch of holy indignation. Up to now, "He had borne the Devil's insults and temptations with singular patience; He had replied to him with mildness and gentleness," says Timpson in his work on *The Angels of God,* published in 1845, "but now the blasphemous audacity could no longer be endured: the holiness of the Redeemer obliged Him to show His resentment, and exert His power to rid Himself of so vile a creature," as He did when He commanded, *Get thee hence, Satan!*

Milton describes how this once choicest of all the glorious seraphs was:

> . . . Brighter once amidst the host
> of Angels, than that star the stars among.

Then the poet goes on to speak of his fall:

> Satan, so call him now; his former name
> Is heard no more in Heaven: he of the first,
> If not the first archangel; great in power
> In favour and pre-eminence.

This created but superhuman angelic being is represented in Scripture as the avowed adversary of the Triune God of Scripture, of the

Saints, and of all ennobling virtues. The name *Satan* means "adversary," and the Apostles thought of him in this way (Gal. 6:17; John 2:15–17). Peter, in particular, centers on Satan's ferocity as an enemy when he warns us to "Be sober, be vigilant; because your adversary the devil, as a roaring lion, walketh about, seeking whom he may devour" (1 Peter 5:8). Mark, in his reference to the temptation, says that "Jesus was with the wild beasts." Those wild beasts, though perhaps made more ferocious at that time by "the roaring lion" himself, could not harm Jesus, co-Creator of the beasts of the field. They knew that He could calm them as He did for Daniel.

By His victory over the wild beasts, and the Beast himself, Jesus regained for man the empire over the beasts which the First Adam lost. "The wolf shall dwell with the lamb, and the leopard shall lie down with the kid. . . . They shall not hurt nor destroy in all my holy mountain" (Isa. 11:6, 9).

As *Satan*, then, such an adversary stands in his true character, and Jesus no longer deals with him as a pretended friend and pious counselor, but calls him by his right name—His knowledge of which from the outset He had carefully concealed till now—and orders him off. The truth Satan heard, that allegiance is due to God and to Him only, Peter had to learn when he sought to turn his Master from the appointed path of suffering. Unconsciously, the apostle became the mouthpiece of the tempter, and he had the sorrow of hearing himself rebuked with the self-same words of the third temptation, "Get thee behind me, Satan" (Matt. 16:23). But the use of such a command for the first time in the wilderness implies that in all previous temptations "The Wicked One" has presented himself in disguise, but now he is revealed in all his nakedness and absolute antagonism to the divine will.

As we come now to the three temptations of the Incarnate One by Satan, their nature can be compared to John's description of the three classes of sins in the world (see 1 John 2:16):

The lust of the flesh. The first temptation (Matt. 4:1–4).

The lust of the eye. The second temptation (Matt. 4:5–7).

The pride of life. The third temptation (Matt. 4:8–11).

These three direct attacks of the adversary require our close and reverent attention, seeing they were designed to induce Jesus to act from Himself and totally independently of His Father, and of the Holy Spirit. The first two temptations were efforts by the devil to force Jesus to abuse His miraculous powers to prove that He was the Son of God. Sinless though He was, His hunger made Him susceptible to feel the *first* temptation. Because believing, He felt the *second*; and because of His great love and pity for mankind, He was emotionally affected by the third.

The First Temptation

This initial temptation was one to distrust. It was personal and associated with the body, or the natural, physical life of Jesus. The phrase, "He was afterward an hungered," supplies the purpose of the devil's first assault. *Fasting* can mean a spare diet, such as John the Baptist practiced, for Jesus said of him that he came "neither eating nor drinking." Yet he had his "locusts and wild honey." Or fasting can imply total abstinence from food, which is likely what the fast for forty days and forty nights entailed. While absorbed with the contemplation of the great task He was now facing, Jesus did not find the need for food (see Mark 3:20, 21 and John 4:31, 32). But when those days were over, and the strain of thought and prayer ceased, Jesus found Himself helpless and feeble through want of bodily sustenance, and it was then, when He was physically most unfit to resist, that the strong enemy came.

It is clearly seen that the tempter adapted his strategy to the circumstances of the hour, namely, when Jesus was keenly feeling the craving of hunger. He had unlimited power of working miracles as is seen when, later on, He took a few small loaves and fishes and fed thousands of very hungry people who had gathered to hear Him. So why not make bread for Himself? In effect, the devil said, "If it is right to feed others who are hungry, why is it wrong to feed yourself? If you are a miracle-worker, command these stones to become bread to meet your need for food." Such reasoning implied, "If you do not take this matter into your own hands, you're a dead man."

Perhaps we do not realize sufficiently that the worst temptations are those associated with seemingly harmless actions; and as Richard

Glover points out, "One of the greatest lessons which we need to learn in this life is this: every act is wrong which is done from wrong motives, however innocent in itself it may seem to be."[6] Thus, in this first temptation, the only wrong in the act would be the feelings prompting it.

The devil called upon Jesus to *command* the stones at His feet be made bread, but no command would have been necessary for He could have as easily made those stones into loaves, as He changed water into wine without any word or visible action on His part. He just willed the transformation to take place.

> When Christ at Cana's feast by power divine
> Inspired cold water with the warmth of wine
> See! cried they, while in reddening tide it gushed,
> The bashful stream hath seen its Good and blushed.

Such a silent change would have been the same with the stones becoming bread, but had Jesus yielded to the satanic suggestion He would have taken Himself out of God's hands and made Himself unlike His brethren whose bodily nature He had taken. Man needs a Savior to stand with him in his need, and to teach him how to endure temptation and how to trust. Jesus would not have been such a Savior had He yielded to the devil. And so:

> He who nourished crowds with bread
> Would not one meal unto Himself afford.

We have already indicated that Jesus never performed a miracle for self-advantage, or used spiritual power to supply His own material needs. Had He done so He would have forsaken that reliance upon God which was the primary condition of His assumption of our humanity. "The simple doing for His own comfort what the poor and needy could not do, would have cut the link that unites Him to us. So that act, in itself harmless, would, in the circumstances, have severed Him at once from God and from man."[7] It was alone for the good of others that

---

[6] Glover, *Teacher's Commentary*, 29.
[7] Ibid., 30.

miraculous power was entrusted to Jesus, and the Gospels confirm His strict economy of such power. The aspect, then, of this first temptation was designed to force Him to forsake the nature of man in which He had come to live, die, and rise again—and He rejected it.

It will be further observed that the first two temptations begin with the same formula, namely, "If thou be the Son of God" (Matt. 4:3, 6). *If* suggests doubt, but the devil had no doubt whatever as to the true identity of Jesus as the only Begotten of the Father. Just before the wilderness conflict the Father bore witness, not only to Christ's Messiahship, but also to His eternal, Divine Sonship: "My beloved Son" (Matt. 3:17). But here the devil seems to challenge this adulation by urging Jesus to prove the reality of such a blessed Sonship. Making bread out of stones and leaping from the pinnacle of the temple were to be crucial experiments of this Sonship—efforts to dislodge from His heart the consciousness of His relation to the Father. But the devil did not require the exhibition of these acts as evidence of Christ's Sonship, for from the dateless past, he knew Him to be equal with God.

That the same is equally true of all evil spirits, or fallen angels, is clear from the cure of the demoniac (Mark 1:21–28). In the synagogue at Capernaum in which Jesus had been authoritatively teaching truths causing the worshipers to be astonished, there was a man with an unclean spirit or demon. Alas! this was not the first time or the last an evil spirit possessed a pew-holder. The character of impurity is ascribed to evil spirits some twenty times in the Gospels. As Jesus came to expel this particular spirit from the man possessed, he cried out, "Let us alone; what have we to do with thee, thou Jesus of Nazareth?: art thou come to destroy us? I know thee who thou art, the Holy One of God" (Mark 1:24).

No wonder the agent of the devil said, "What have we to do with thee?" Jesus had nothing in common with hell. The question implied the entire separation of interests and values between the Holy One of God and unclean spirits. The reaction of the demon to its expulsion from the man presents a striking feature of the miracle, namely, that of the testimony of the powers of darkness to the deity and humanity of our Lord.

Jesus of Nazareth. This was the current designation of those who held Him in honor (Luke 18:37). Looking upon His human form, all could see that the unclean spirit used this title describing Him as a man, born in Nazareth. But then, in a remarkable way, there follows the confirmation of hell on the Messiahship of Jesus, and its strictest meaning:

The Holy One of God. "The Holy One" (Ps. 16:10), the One who had attained the highest form of holiness and divinity. He was, indeed, the God-Man.

The rebuke and command of Jesus aroused the rage of the unclean spirit who knew only too well that the Holy One he faced was also the One unafraid of the devil and his apostate angels. When Jesus said, "Hold thy peace!" He literally said, "Be muzzled or gagged." This is the same verb used of the calming of the winds and the waves (Mark 4:39). What a display of deity this expulsion was! The people were amazed at His authority and power, and quickly the fame of Jesus spread abroad claiming that evil spirits were forced to obey Him. By His incarnation, Jesus sealed the doom of the devil and his evil hosts (John 12:31; 16:11, R.V.).

As for the devil, although he was a liar and the father of lies (John 8:44), instead of saying, "If thou art the Son of God," he could have truthfully confessed: "I know thee who thou art, the Holy One of God," for he knew Him only too well. At the creation of the angelic host by the Trinity, it is clearly evident that the devil, a created being, was not created a devil, but as one endowed with position, dignity, and honor. Phrases used of him (such as, "Day star, son of the morning"; "the anointed cherub that covereth"; "perfect in beauty") can only apply to the highest of all angelic beings (Gen. 3:24; Job 38:7).

Does it not seem as if the dominion of this world, as it was originally created, was given to the devil while he was yet a holy angel (a position Jesus Himself recognized when He called him, "The prince of this world," John 12:31; 14:30; 16:11)? But the catastrophe overtaking God's original creation, as given in Genesis 1–2, came as the result of his rebellion in heaven. From Isaiah 45:18, it is apparent that the earth was not originally "without form and void," but became so as the result of a terrible upheaval; and the remainder of the first chapter in the Bible is the record of the production of *cosmos* out of *chaos*, to fit it for its new inhabitants and rulers (Gen. 1:26–28). The Apocrypha has it, "Through envy of the Devil came death into the world, for his only chance of retaining dominion lay in making man a rebel like himself, which he did when the First Adam disobeyed a Divine command."

But in a past Eternity when all was perfect bliss and harmony, the devil, before he became a devil, praised and honored the Three Persons of the Blessed Trinity. All His angels praised Him (Ps. 148:2). Receiving their praises was the Only Begotten of the Father, as well as the Father Himself, and "the son of the morning" joined in those praises to the eternal Son of God. Thus the devil knew all about the wonderful love and union that had existed between the Father and the Son, and he also knew Him as God's well-beloved Son only too well. Being heaven-born, he had beheld the full effulgence of glory surrounding Him, of whom the Father said, "I have begotten thee."

Then God proclaimed His Son to be His *Generalissimo*, with Himself as Supreme Ruler in heaven and earth, and Lucifer as under-ruler over creation. Can it be that because he expected the post of honor assigned to God the Son, so becoming next in honor, majesty, and power to God the Supreme, that then his hatred for the Son was born? The murderous hatred toward Jesus that burned in the hearts of the Pharisees was born of the arch-hater of Jesus, namely, the devil. Without fear, He told those who sought to kill Him that they were children of the Devil (John 8:44). What is so instructive, however, about Jesus during His contact with the devil, was the comfort He found for His own heart in Scripture, and likewise the answers it provided Him to the satanic suggestions presented.

"It is Written"—is there not the air of irrevocability or finality about this three-word declaration given to the devil three times by Jesus? Scripture is irreversible. Pilate's irrevocable dictum is far truer of the revelation of God: "What I have written, I have written" (John 19:22). Scripture is God's complete, final and unalterable Word to the world with its original copy in heaven (see Prov. 30:5, 6; Dan. 10:21; Gal. 3:8; Jude 3; Rev. 22:18, 19). God's Word is indestructible. Man may try to destroy it, as Jehoiakim sought to do with his penknife (Jer. 36:23), but he can never succeed, because the Written Word, like the Living Word Himself, liveth and abideth forever.

In His response to the overtures of the devil, Jesus has left us an example that we should follow in His steps. If we, too, would be victorious over the wiles of the devil, we must know how to use the

Sword of the Spirit, which is the Word of God. Jesus did not enter into the pros and cons of each proposal of the devil, but in each case He just quoted a passage of Scripture, and the tempter was silenced. Jesus lived in the will of God as revealed in the Word of God, and thus defeated the enemy. Being saturated in Scripture, as He was, reveals, as Griffith Thomas expresses it:

1. Principles involved in given situation;
2. Speciousness of temptation, whether of self or of Satan;
3. Shallowness of life resulting from yielding.

In union with the Scripture-loving Lord, we, too, can be more than conquerors over the world, the flesh, and the devil (John 15:5).

Our Lord's first apt choice of a verse to meet the subtle suggestion of the devil reveals His identity with the humanity of which He became part, and for whose salvation He gave Himself. As a Man, He felt the pangs of hunger, but yet said, "*Man* shall not live by bread *alone*" (Matt. 4:4; Deut. 8:3). Even the Son of Man Himself needed material substance for the body, but spiritual food was for Him a prime and prior necessity. With Job of old He could confess: "Neither have I gone back from the commandment of his lips; I have esteemed the words of his mouth more than my necessary food" (23:12).

Because of the constitution of the body, material food is necessary for existence, but man has a soul requiring spiritual sustenance; and because the soul has precedence over the body, in the spiritual realm, food for the soul has the preeminence. Thus the experience of Jesus in the wilderness clothed the history of the bread from heaven for Israel with a new significance. "*Every* word that proceedeth out of the mouth of God" implies that Scripture, as a whole, is the miracle-working Word of God. The First Adam had every tree of the garden for food, but yet he fell; the Last Adam had only desert stones to mock His hunger, yet He conquered His foe.

The blessed truth, then, emerging from this first temptation is that as the Son of God with power, Jesus could have made bread out of stones to satisfy His hunger and sustain His physical life. By the exercise of such a power He could reveal that He was the conscious possessor of miraculous gifts. But had He yielded to the request of the devil, He would have been guilty of self-assertion and distrust, and also of the denial of the Sonship recently affirmed at His baptism (Matt. 3:16, 17). As to His initial use of Scripture against the Devil, no Old Testament passage could have been so appropriate to His purpose as the one He chose from Deuteronomy. It was as if He argued with His own heart in this way, suggested by Faussett's *Comments*:

> Now, if Israel spent, not forty days, but forty years in a waste, howling wilderness, where there were no means of human subsistence, not starving, but divinely provided for, on purpose to prove to every age that human support depends not upon bread, but upon God's unfailing word of promise and pledge of all needful providential care, am I, distrusting this word of God, and despairing of relief, to take the law into my own hand? True, the Son of God is able enough to turn stones into bread: but what the Son of God is able to do is not the present question, but what is *man's duty* under want of the necessaries of life. And as Israel's condition in the wilderness did not justify their unbelieving murmurings and frequent desperation, so neither would mine warrant the exercise of the power of the Son of God in snatching despairingly at unwarranted relief. As man, therefore, I will await divine supply, nothing doubting that at the fitting time it will arrive.[8]

The Second Temptation

Though He was the Sinless One, extreme hunger caused Jesus to feel the first temptation, but because of His obedience to God and His Word He deeply felt this second assault of the enemy, which had a national character. Having assailed Jesus through *His bodily sufferings* and seen Him yet victorious by faith, the devil now endeavors to make such faith overdo itself in presumption, and so he appeals now to *His spiritual exaltation.*

"The devil taketh him"—just how the tempter took Jesus up to the high place of the Temple in the holy city—the metropolis of all Jewish worship—we are not told. Whatever shape of personality or substance the devil possessed is beyond our present knowledge. The consistent

---

[8] Robert Jamieson, A. R. Faussett, and David Brown, *J.F.B. Complete Commentary* (Peabody: Hendrickson Publishers, 1996) 12.

truth of Scripture is that he is a personal devil and can assume borrowed shapes and subtle transformation to achieve his evil purposes, just as he used Peter to dissuade his Master from going to the cross. Are we not warned never to be ignorant of his clever devices?

"If thou be the Son of God"—this further temptation starts from the attestation of the character of Jesus as the Son of God—a Sonship He constantly affirmed. He was always determined not to be disputed out of this affirmation, even by the son of perdition, who knew only too well the eternal relationship between the Father and the Son. Had He succumbed to the wiles of the devil, then He would have become a prodigal son, and unworthy of becoming the Savior of the World.

"Cast thyself down"—early church literature records a curious coincidence that James the Just, the brother of Jesus, was thrown down from a high platform of the temple into one of the courts below and was crushed to death (*Eusebius, H.E.* 2.23). It would have been the same fate for Jesus without any miraculous intervention. The lofty position overlooking the temple courts was a most convenient point from which a multitude could be addressed, so the devil suggested to Jesus that He should preach to the gathered multitudes below from this great height, then prove His Messianic claims beyond all question by flying through the air and reaching the ground unharmed. But had Jesus jumped from the lofty pulpit as a *Man* without resource to His own inherent power of natural forces for a safe, unharmed landing, He would have been killed after hitting the stone pavement. This shortcut to acceptance by the people would be welcomed by them, and it was this commended to Jesus by the devil as being quite safe, easy, and effective, with a Scripture promise guaranteeing a delightful flight and victorious landing. Thus, as Dummelow's *Commentary* summarizes this satanic approach:

> Stripped of its symbolic form, this was a temptation to take a short and easy road to recognition as the Messiah by giving "a sign from Heaven" which even the most incredulous and unspiritual would be compelled to accept. This short and easy method Jesus decisively rejected. He determined to appeal to the spiritual apprehension of mankind, that they might believe on Him, not because they were astounded by His miracles, and could not resist their evidence, but

because they were attracted by the holiness and graciousness of His character, by the loftiness of His teaching, and by the love of God to man which was manifested in all His words and actions. He intended His miracles to be secondary, an aid to the faith of those who on other grounds were inclined to believe, but not portents to extort the adhesion of those who had no sympathy with Himself or His aims.[9]

For ourselves, the lesson at this point is obvious. The same temptation comes to us when a sinister voice urges us to take liberties with God; or to parade our virtues; or to pursue any course morally perilous, in the idea that God will intervene and keep us from being destroyed. Many who do not fall through despair fall through presumption, pride rendering the temptation more seductive.

But is there not a further interpretation of this second temptation for us to consider? While Satan tried to persuade Jesus to throw Himself down, he could not push Him down. Yet was this not another effort to kill Him before the death of the cross He willed but the Devil did not want, seeing that by His death and resurrection his own fate would be sealed? That he bore intense hatred for God's beloved Son from the beginning of his evil career forms a great and important subject of Bible study.

From the first proclamation of the redemption evangel declaring that the seed of the woman would bruise the serpent's head, Satan, symbolized as *the serpent*, set about the destruction of *The Seed Royal* from which Jesus was to come, and almost succeeded. Many devices and arts were conceived to exterminate the Seed that would ultimately produce his great Antagonist and Glorious Conqueror. If ever the devil and his angels had a bad day, it was on the day that Jesus was "born of a woman," the realization of the promise that her seed would destroy the authority and power of the devil. Here was a marvel—a Child divinely conceived and born, and all at once the devil's murderous energies are aroused, and his subtle wisdom used for the attempt to

---

[9]J. R. Dummelow, *A Commentary on the Holy Bible* (New York: The Macmillen Co., 1942) 633.

slaughter Mary's renowned Infant under Herod's edict to kill all help-less babies.

As we know, the Holy Babe was divinely spared, but the enemy was bent on further murderous attacks, and this present temptation appears to be one of them. By His sudden appearance in the temple, Jesus would obtain power and popularity, and as to any possibility of destroying Himself in descending, had not God promised angelic guardianship? But this device to identify Jesus with vainglory, spectacular fame, and distrust was thwarted by One Stronger than he.

Later on, the startling word was brought to Jesus, "Herod will kill thee." But poor Herod was but the devil's tool, and his foxlike character, reflected in the knavish craftiness of the Pharisees, was a gift of the devil. But the death edict of Herod met the challenge, "Go ye, and tell that fox (that) . . . I must walk today, and tomorrow, and the day following" (Luke 13:32, 33). In effect, "Tell the devil and his demons that I am immortal till my work is done." Then we have phrases like, "(They) consulted how they might take Jesus by subtlety and kill Him" (Matt. 26:4). " . . . took counsel . . . how they might destroy him" (Mark 3:6). " . . . that they might cast him down headlong" (Luke 4:29). "Ye seek to kill me" (John 8:37). "They took up stones to cast at him" (John 8:59; 10:31–39).

Jesus, however, had to die, but it was a death ordained of God—a death by which He was to destroy death forever. " . . . through death he might destroy him that had the power of death, that is, the devil" (Heb. 2:14). All his premature efforts to kill Jesus *before* the cross failed, simply because it had been decreed that He should die *on* the cross. It is thus that His death at Calvary differs from all other deaths. Others *suffer* death—Jesus *achieved* it. Death comes to cut short the life of humans and frustrate their aims and ambitions, but Jesus, by His death, consummated, crowned, and completed His work. Hence His triumphant cry as He expired: "*It is finished!*" (John 19:30).

The devil's last great attempt to destroy God's magnificent and perfect plan of redemption was to make sure that Jesus *remained* dead. So the sepulchre was made secure, the stone sealed, and guards set to watch it. But this effort to keep that sacred and scarred body sealed in a tomb was defeated for "Death could not keep its prey," and so on the third day He arose, "A Victor o'er the dark domain." How our devil-beset hearts are continuously comforted by His own words, "I am he that liveth, and was dead; and behold, I am alive for evermore, Amen: and have the keys of hell and of death" (Rev. 1:18).

1. Satan and Scripture

Satanic subtlety in this second temptation is found in the tempter's use of Scripture. Was there not a seeming warrant for the dramatic, crucial test of Sonship in the declaration of the psalmist that angelic hosts would bear up, or surround, or protect God's chosen One from danger or death (Ps. 91:11, 12)? Satan's quotation, as far as it went, was in harmony with the Hebrew original, but what he cunningly omitted from the promise was the phrase, "To keep thee in all thy ways," for he knew, only too well, that had Jesus succumbed to his appeal it would not have been one of *His ways.*

Saintly, stately Bishop Joseph Hall, upon reading of the devil's use of Scripture in the early 16th century, exclaimed: "But what is this I see? Satan himself with a Bible in under his arm and a text in his mouth!" When he is seen thus, it is to no good purpose, for he is pastmaster at using, or misusing, Scripture to his own advantage. Satan is a theologian. He approached Jesus craftily and is the father of all who handle the Word of God deceitfully (2 Cor. 4:2). How able is he to pervert and obscure the true significance of Scripture (Matt. 13:25)! It is apparent that stung by the defeat of his first endeavor to tempt Jesus through the power of the Word of God, the devil was eager to try the effect of Scripture from his own mouth (see 2 Cor. 11:13–15).

2. Jesus and Scripture

Satan's thrust was made noneffective by the way Jesus handled the same weapon of spiritual warfare, the Sword of the Spirit. Jesus said, "It is written." He did not reply by filling in for the devil, then quoting part of the portion he used. Jesus knew that he had omitted, "To keep thee in all thy ways," and also the latter part of the same divine promise: "Thou shalt tread upon the lion and the adder" (Ps. 91:13). With great calm, however, He broke the force of this satanic onslaught by quoting another Scripture, for the entire Word of God was known to Him.

From the answer of Jesus, it is evident that the devil designed to urge Him to prove that He was the Son of God, and that His Father would send angels for His preservation. As we have already suggested, he sought to destroy Jesus. He would have gladly hurled Him from the parapet, to a frightful death below, but he dared not to make the attempt for he knew that the One before him was "stronger than he." Thus he resorted to the course of presumption, but Jesus perceived his evil intent and meekly replied for His rebuke, "Thou shalt not tempt the Lord thy God" (Deut. 6:16).

Jesus promised that when the Holy Spirit came as His ascension gift, one aspect of His ministry would be to bring to the remembrance of the believer the truths of Holy Writ. But He Himself had no need of this specific office of the Spirit, for in Him, the Written Word and the Living Word were one. The simple "It is written" implies that Jesus meant in His reply to the Devil, "True, the Scripture you have quoted, and so it is written, and on that promise I implicitly rely; but in using it there is another Scripture which you must not forget." This particular Scripture He quoted has a special historical reference, "Ye shall not tempt the Lord your God, as ye tempted him in Massah" (Deut. 6:16).

The specific sin of the people at Massah was their unwillingness to believe the presence of God was actual until they saw a supernatural evidence of it. Thus, the question they asked sprang from their unbelief, "Is Jehovah among us or not?" In using this Scripture, then, Jesus implied, as He related it to Himself, that to demand a proof of God's care in the way the devil suggested would have identified Him with a like spirit of distrust Massah had manifested. One lesson Jesus learned as a *Man* was to commit Himself absolutely to His Father's will—which committal led Him to refuse the aid of twelve legions of angels the Father would have gladly sent for His Son's protection (Matt. 26:53). Jamieson's *Commentary* observes:

> Preservation in danger is divinely pledged: shall I then *create* danger, either to put the promised security skeptically to the proof, or wantonly to demand a display of it? That were "to tempt the Lord my God," which, being expressly forbidden, would forfeit the right to expect preservation.[10]

---

[10] Jamieson, et. al., *Commentary*, 14.

There is an aspect of this second temptation, however, that seems to lay hold of my mind with an irresistible force, namely, that it provides a further evidence of Jesus as "God manifest in flesh." In respect to *His humanity*, He was still suffering from the pangs of physical suffering He refused to avoid in a miraculous way. Also, it was as a *Man* that He was being tempted in all points as ordinary men are, but never yielding to temptation as even the best of men do. As for an expression of *His deity*, He ever was the Son of God, but in the verse He quoted to the devil who was tempting *Him*, He applied the words to Himself and said to him, "*Ye* shall not tempt (Me) the Lord *thy* God." Think of it, "thy God!" Yes, Jesus was even the devil's God, for although he was as a roaring lion prowling around to devour, he was but a lion on a leash and could not go beyond divine permission, evidenced by the command used in the next temptation, "Get thee hence, Satan!" That was the fiat of the *God-Man*.

The central lesson for our hearts is obvious. We are forbidden to experiment with God. As Richard Glover expresses it in his volume on *Matthew*:

> *Jesus will take no liberties with God*—will expect angels to protect Him in every way on which God sends Him; will not ask, dare not expect them, to protect Him in running needless risks from motives of spiritual pride. Too often we take liberties; sinning willfully, in the hope that, after all, grace will not be withdrawn; or going into temptation and risking safety of soul, in the hope that some angel will prevent mischief. Learn the Saviour's way: "No liberties with God," no self-display. The lowly path of duty is to be preferred to the ostentatious path of seeming faith. Remember the solemn words of Moses: *The soul that doth aught presumptuously . . . shall be cut off from among his people*, Num. 15:30.[11]

The Third Temptation

Because of the expectation of the sudden, spectacular appearance of the Messiah in the temple (Mal. 3:1), the previous temptation had a national aspect, whereas, the temptation now before us, being asso-

---

[11] Glover, *Teacher's Commentary*, 31–32.

ciated with the kingdoms of this world, bears an international or universal distinction. Further, this was not another temptation of ambition, but to a lower standard of spiritual work by spiritual means, and so Jesus rejected it, not because His right to rulership over the world was wrong but because the longer and harder way He was taking to become the King of Kings *via* the cross was the only right way.

In effect Satan said, "You want to control the world, then take a shortcut—avoid the cross, and accept the throne on easy terms. Do evil that good may come of it. Employ carnal weapons in a spiritual warfare." But this grandiose and final approach, like the previous ones, signally failed in its design. Evil had presented itself in disguise, making sins of distrust appear as acts of faith, while now it showed itself in its naked and absolute antagonism to the divine will.

It may be fitting at this point to consider the power with which, by virtue of his seraphic origin, he was vested—before he became a devil, and of which he boasted in his declared ownership of the kingdom of this world. In Luke's record of the wilderness experience of Jesus, he cites the devil as adding, "For that is delivered unto me, and to whomsoever I will give it" (4:6), and the language of Jesus and that of His apostles appears to support his claim. To Jesus, he was, "the prince of this world" (John 12:31; 14:30; 16:11). Jesus did not deny that he had the right to make such an offer, or that he had the power to fulfill it. He simply refused to accept the rulership of the world on the devil's terms. Then Paul describes him as "the god of this world" and as "the prince of the power of the air" (2 Cor. 4:4; Eph. 2:2). As for his hosts they are "the world rulers of this present darkness" (Eph. 6:12).

When the world was originally created, Lucifer, as the devil then was in his unfallen state, was granted the rulership of the world. With his rebellion, however, when he aspired to be as a *God*, chaos overtook the original creation and it became "without form and void" as the result of such a terrible catastrophe (Gen. 1:2; Isa. 45:18). Cosmos, however, came out of chaos to fit it for its new inhabitants and rulers (Gen. 1:26–28). But almost immediately the enemy began his devilish work in the world, and he could be restrained only by a superior power, which was promised in the first announcement of God's purpose in the incarnation of His Son (Gen. 3:14, 15).

We cannot doubt that with his fall from heaven, the Devil lost much of the rectitude and glory and power of his angelic nature; and that, when he first commenced as the *devil*, God placed upon him the chains of restraint as the badge of apostasy. He never possessed the divine attributes of omnipotence, omniscience and omnipresence; and thus he functioned under general prohibition to do anything to the prejudice of creation, or to act anything by force or violence without divine permission. Although the prince of demons, with hell at his command, and power as a roaring lion to devour, the devil is a lion locked up in the tower of the divine will, and thus he is unable to inflict the hurt he wishes, or indeed any hurt at all. Through the victory Jesus secured over the devil in the wilderness, and by His death and resurrection, every child of God has the authority to challenge his approach in temptation and say, "Get thee behind me, Satan!" and, thereby, overcome him.

All that the devil was originally granted was the *oversight* of the kingdoms of this world, but not the *ownership* of them, so true to his character as a deceiver he offered Jesus, as a gift, something he did not own. Hezekiah distinctly declared, "Thou art the God, even thou alone, of all the kingdoms of the earth" (2 Kings 19:15). As for David, he likewise affirmed that the Lord's kingdom "ruleth over all" (Ps. 103:19). The devil, then, not only usurped his authority, but reached the limit of his pride, when as a apostate angel he not only offered Jesus ownership of a possession he did not own, but sought to persuade Him, the Lord of Angels, to bow down and recognize him as a deity. Here was the devil of a god, seeking to induce "the very God of very God" to become a devil-worshipper! To have Jesus bow down and worship him would have been the master stroke of his blasphemy.

As for the tempted One Himself, He could afford to despise the offer of the devil, for He knew that through His conquest of him, "the kingdoms of this world are the kingdoms of our Lord" (Rev. 11:15). The grand purpose of the incarnation was that Jesus should have an everlasting kingdom of grace and glory (Luke 1:33). Concerning this third temptation Ellicott's *Commentary* observes:

> The offer made by the Tempter rested upon the apparent evidence of the world's history. The rulers of the world, the Herods and its

Caesars, seemed to have obtained their eminence by trampling the laws of God under foot, and accepting Evil in the Lord and Master of the World . . . In this case the temptation is no longer addressed to the sense of Sonship, but to the love of power. To be a King like other kings, mighty to deliver His people from their oppressors, and achieve the glory which the prophets had predicted for the Christ; this was possible for Him if only He would go beyond the self-imposed limits of accepting whatsoever His Father ordered for Him.

In His reply, Jesus tore the mask from "the enemy, who had assumed the fairest form to do the foulest deed," and commanded him to beat a hasty retreat—which he did, leaving Jesus for a season. *Get thee hence, Satan*! Here He used the devil's most common alias, which is his invariable name in the Old Testament, and occurs some fifty times. *Satan* means "the adversary," and he has ever been the chief and persistent adversary of the Written Word, of Jesus the Living Word, of the Father, and of the Holy Spirit (Gal. 5:17; 1 John 2:15–17). But this satanic Goliath met his defeat at the hand of David's Son and Lord when He used a single pebble from the brook of the Bible. Timpson, in his most valuable work on *The Angels of God*, has the quotation from Bennett's *Lectures*:

Having lifted up his heel, and stamped upon the serpent; he who had pretended to have worlds at his command, and to be able to promote Christ Himself to honour, is now seen a poor vanquished, degraded foe, writhing under the foot of the Conqueror. He who had defeated the first Adam, in the full strength of innocence in Paradise, is himself conquered by the Last Adam, when starving in a desert.[12]

It will be observed that Jesus took no notice of the pomposity of the devil, in vainly offering kingdoms for His homage, and by His attitude teaches us that it is most dangerous to parley with temptation, or to estimate seeming advantages which necessitate a violent duty to

[12] Timpson, *Angels*, 410.

the Lord our God. In the rebuke of Jesus, we also witness His power over even the chief of the fallen angels by the powerful Sword of the Spirit (Eph. 6:17).

"It is written"—yet again Jesus silenced the devil by the quotation of another appropriate text. The Scripture with which He parted with him was Deuteronomy 6:13, and proves that His unfailing armory of defense in His contest and conquest was the divinely inspired Word of God. Three times over He answered the devil with "*It is written.*" He never argued or reasoned, but He simply quoted Scripture for in its commands and counsels, precepts and promises. He had weapons of war mighty through God to the pulling down of the stronghold of the enemy. He defeated Satan by the means open to His humblest follower.

The apt passage Jesus chose as His answer reads, "Thou shalt worship the Lord thy God, and him only shalt thou serve" (Luke 4:8). What a crushing blow this dealt the tempter! He had demanded that Jesus worship him, an apostate angel who, in his unfallen state, worshipped God. Thus, the word *worship* used here emphasized emphatically that what the tempter claimed was precisely what God had forbidden. As for the word *only*, does it not bring out most strongly the *negative* and prohibitory feature of the divine command? On the word *serve*, Ellicott comments that "it is never used by the LXX of any but religious service; and in this sense conclusively it is used in the New Testament, as we find it here."

The Bible gave Jesus His light and answer, and so He bade Satan, "Get thee hence." He never looked for one moment at the delightful prospects the enemy presented, but only at the *dubious means.* Jesus was resolved to go uncrowned as ruler of "all the kingdoms" till God crowned Him; and to employ no art but *love* to win the empire of mankind. Does His example not teach us that proper influence will come, if we deserve to have it; and to seek no power save that which naturally grows out of the consecrated service we are able to render for the spiritual benefit of others?

Was there not a sense in which the *Man* Christ Jesus facing Satan was *The Lord thy God?* Was He not born as "Christ the Lord," and did not Mary say of the Holy Child she was about to bear, "My soul doth magnify the Lord, And my spirit hath rejoiced in God my Saviour" (Luke 1:46)? As for being the object of worship, Jesus as God manifest in flesh never refused it. The wise men fell down and worshipped Him when He was only a young child, but when he became a Man, several are spoken of as worshipping Him during the three years of His public ministry (see Matt. 2:11; 8:2; 9:18; 15:25; 28:9, 17; etc.). Thus, in effect Jesus rebuked Satan by saying, "You blasphemously ask *Me* to worship *you*? Before your rebellion in heaven, along with the angelic host, you worshipped Me as the Son of God, but when you transferred such worship to yourself, you prepared the way to ask *Me* as the Son of Man to worship *you*. But demons and men alike must remember that I, only, as the Word made flesh, have the right to claim worship and adoration. Worship thou Me."

Temptation Was Outward

It is essential to emphasize a most important aspect of our Lord's temptations. They were all external. As Professor Plummer expresses it: "The change of scene is mental . . . the glory of all the kingdoms of the world could be suggested to the mind . . . What these words do imply is that the temptations came to Him from the outside." There was nothing internal to which Satan could appeal. Satan could enter into Judas seeing he already possessed a foothold in his traitorous heart. But the tempter could approach Jesus only from without, and so his temptations rebounded simply because there was no congenial soil in His sinless heart in which they could fructify. Jesus was internally and externally holy and conformed to the precepts of Scripture.

As the Son of God, He left a sinless world intrinsically holy, but as the Son of man He found Himself in a sinful world. During His sojourn on earth He remained perfectly holy. The reason for this was the fact that He was born *holy*, that is, with no inherited evil propensities. In announcing His birth to Mary the Archangel Gabriel said, "That *holy* thing that shall be born of thee shall be called the Son of God" (Luke 1:35). Native sinfulness or "original sin" was not inherited by Jesus, who, from His conception in Mary's womb to His cross, remained, "holy, harmless, undefiled, separate from sinners" because He was "made higher than the heavens" (Heb. 7:26).

Born with only one nature, namely, an unsinning nature, Jesus, tempted to the full as a Man, emerged from the conflict "without sin," or without being prompted to yield by the pressure of any evil nature

within His assumed form. To His persistent, satanically inspired enemies, the Pharisees, He could say, "Which of you convinceth Me of
sin?" (John 8:46). Peter declared of Him whose example we are to
emulate, "Who did not sin" (1 Peter 2:22). Three times over Pilate gave
his verdict concerning the innocency of Jesus, "I find no fault in him"
(Luke 23:4, 14, 22). Pilate's wife had troubled dreams over this *just
man*. The scribes and Pharisees tempted Jesus over the woman taken
in adultery who, if guilty, merited death by stoning. The pointed reply
routed His foes: "He that is without sin among you, let him first cast
a stone at her" (John 8:7). The only One present "without sin" was
Jesus, but he never raised a stone against the woman, but compassion-
ately wooed her from her harlotry to holiness of life, saying, "Go, and
sin no more" (John 8:11).

But with us it is totally different, for we were "brought forth in
iniquity, and in sin" (Ps. 51:4). David's confession does not imply, as
the ancient rabbis erroneously suggested, that he was born as the result
of his mother's adultery, but represents a statement of truth of experience so constantly affirmed in Scripture of hereditary corruption,
the innate possession of every child of man. The temptations of Jesus
were outward, and ineffective, because there was nothing internal for
them to rely upon for submission.

A truth Lord Bacon taught his own generation, and succeeding
ages, was "that it is not a lie that passes through the mind that does the
harm, but the lie that lodges there." Being holy within there was no
lodgment for the enemy's lies in the heart of Jesus. He was most
explicit in His own admission of immunity from sin when He said to
His disciples, "The prince of this world cometh, and *hath nothing in
me*" (John 14:30, italics mine). There was no territory within Him the
devil could claim. The temptation was a grim reality for Jesus, and He
met the tempter in the strength of His sinless, human nature, assisted
by divine grace. As God, He could not be tempted at all. With us,
however, the wiles of the devil receive a sympathetic consideration
from the old nature we inherited and for which we are not responsible.
Sin and condemnation come when we allow the devil to use this evil
bent within us for our spiritual defeat. Our deep depravity of nature
is enough to make angels weep, but their sorrow is greater when we
allow the devil to successfully use it to prevent holiness of life. Paul

(who had known the Lord for many years and had been in the third heaven), must have been conscious of this danger when he penned such verses as:

"What I would, that I do not . . .
In me (that is, in my flesh) dwelleth no good thing . . .
It is no more I (the new man in Christ) that do it, but
sin (the old man in Adam) that dwelleth in me" (Rom. 7:15–25).

The apostle, however, found a glorious deliverance from this "body of death . . . through Jesus Christ our Lord." Jesus, then, had one nature, namely, an unsinning nature; but the saints possess a dual nature—the old corrupt nature, condemned by God, and the new nature received from the Holy Spirit in regeneration. Our responsibility is to have the new nature in the ascendancy and ever victorious over the old nature (1 John 2:13, 14, 16, 29).

After Satan—the Seraphs

Matthew provides us with a striking conclusion to his account of our Lord's temptations: *The devil—the angels.* What extremes! Hell retreats—heaven appears!

"Then the devil leaveth him" (Matt. 4:11).

Are you not arrested by the writer's *Then*? *When* was it that he stopped harrassing Jesus? Why, after he had exhausted all his evil arts for the time being. The devil found our Lord's third thrust of the sharp, two-edged Sword so quick and powerful that, totally defeated, he left Him for a season, or for a further convenient occasion. He is never weary in his evil-doing. Persistently and perseveringly he pursues his prey in the hope of a final capture. As Bishop Jeremy Taylor remarked in his *Life of Christ*—"If he could ever have spied a time of returning he wanted not will or malice to observe and use it."[13]

---

[13] Jeremy Taylor, *The Life of Our Blessed Saviour Jesus Christ* (Philadelphia: D. Dickenson, 1819).

Luke puts it, "When the devil had ended all the temptation he departed from him for a season" (4:13). The contest was not finally over, but renewed from time to time as in the passionate statement of Peter, "Be it far from thee, Lord; this shall not be unto thee" (Matt. 16:22), and in the open enmity of the prince of this world, "Hereafter (Jesus said) I will not talk much with you: for the prince of this world cometh, and with nothing in me" (John 14:30). The definite season here indicated is expressly referred to by Jesus (Luke 22:52, 53; John 14:30). Calvary forever ended satanic attacks upon Him, for His final cry, "It is finished" was the paean of absolute triumph over the devil and his angels.

"Behold, angels came and ministered to Him."

Truly, this was something to "Behold," for after the adversary came the angels! Hell had frowned, but now heaven smiles, succors, and refreshes the heart, and the strain of trial is more than repaired by its gracious ministries. Satan had tempted Jesus by the promise of angelic guardianship in a spectacular attempt to prove his Messiahship. Now, legitimately, the promise *is* fulfilled on behalf of the victorious yet weak and hungry Victor. To what we have already said regarding the ministry of angels, and a following chapter devoted entirely to their relationship with Jesus, perhaps a further word is necessary as to their precise service at the conclusion of His temptations.

Poets and artists have sensualized on the nature of the angelic ministration given. Scripture leaves it undefined. "What is instructive is," says Ellicott, "that the help of their service, the contrast between the calm and beauty of their presence and that of the wild beasts and of the tempter, comes as the reward of the abnegation which refused to make their ministry the subject of an experimental test." The visit of the angels to the weary One must have been of a strengthening and encouraging nature for Luke adds, "Jesus returned in the power of the Spirit in Galilee: and there went out a fame of his through all the region round about. And he taught in their synagogues, being glorified of all" (4:14, 15).

What are some of the lessons for us to take to heart as we leave our absorbing meditation on the evident proof of our Lord's incarnation in His temptation? Uppermost of course was His use of Scripture by which He resisted and overcame Satan. Scripture dwelt within Him richly in all wisdom, and His holy example and conquest in His trial, teaches us that we can overcome "the wicked one" only as we are likewise vigilant and skillful in the use of Scripture.

As we have already seen, Jesus refused to be relieved, even by a miracle which He could have easily wrought, but He continued to endure temptation rather than do what might indicate the least distrust of God. Timpson says:

> While we may, at any time, be tempted to seek relief unlawfully, or to violate duty for the sake of personal gratification, or the advantages of the world, we should remember our Saviour, and cherish the unfeigned faith in the promises of God, which "are all yea and amen in Christ Jesus. We should ever hold fast by the written word of his grace, assured that by the power of his Spirit, or the seasonable visitation of his angels, he will succor and deliver, and save us, even here on earth, and finally to his everlasting kingdom and glory![14]

As Scripture is the inspired and infallible Word of God, may it have a constant home in our memories, affections, and hearts. Let us plead it in prayer which God will notice, approve, and accept! The Holy Oracles are able to form, guide, and preserve right judgment to curb, bind, and regulate our desires, to raise, confirm, and direct our expectations, to silence, enlighten, and purify our consciences, to convict and reprove sin, and make us holy—to make us daily overcomers when assailed by satanic forces.

---

[14] Timpson, *Angels*, 412.

3

HIS VINDICATION

God was manifest in the flesh, justified in the Spirit. (1 Tim. 3:16)

As the Spirit of Wisdom, the Holy Spirit was ever at the side of Christ, Who came as "the wisdom of God," to justify and substantiate all His affirmation and actions. There was the constant vindication of the Spirit against gainsayers, emphasizing that Jesus was who He claimed to be. Before, however, we enter the fascinating study of the remaining brief and poetic lines of this early confession of the Christian faith, which, in the original, are most strikingly set forth, it is important to examine their relative association with the great mystic secret revealed in the second clause, namely, the incarnation of the Son of God: *God manifest in flesh!*

The five impressive and progressive fragments of this triumph-song of the early churches, embracing, as they do, leading facts of the Messianic story, form the enforcement and expansion of the life and labors of Jesus after He was found in fashion as a Man. *The Gospels* and *The Acts* reveal the unfailing vindication by the Spirit of the character, conduct, and claims of Jesus during His days of humiliation: the beatific vision of the angels, the preaching of the Cross, the glorious results of His sacrifice; His return to heaven to the right hand of God. All are but unassailable evidences of the truth that Jesus, as the Word, became flesh and dwelt among men. It is in the light of the Incarnation then, that we approach each of the concluding five lines of the ancient *Confession-Chant*, to adopt Dr. Arthur Way's description of one of the greatest portions of Scripture, 1 Timothy 3:16.

"By Spirit-power was He proved the Just One," is Way's translation of the statement before us, and such proof covers the earthly sojourn of Jesus from His birth to His ascension when, visibly, He left the earth as the God-Man. Strange though it may seem, He received vindication for one of His claims just *before* His birth. When he came among men, He referred quite openly to His *preexistence*—that He did not come into being at His birth, but that He always existed in the bosom of the Father (John 1:1–18). His appearance, thus, as "the Holy Child" was no afterthought with God. Did not Jesus declare that He came from the Father, that "Before Abraham was, I am"? This was an assertion His foes denied and for which they tried to stone Him (John 8:58, 59). Then we have passages like:

"He that came down from heaven" (John 3:13).
"As I came in my Father's name, and ye receive me not" (John 5:43).
"The glory which I had with thee before the world was" (John 17:5).
"Though he was rich, yet for your sakes he became poor" (2 Cor. 8:9).

The *beginning* of John 1:1 goes back into eternity, long before the *beginning* of Genesis 1:1, and prenatal justification of the preexistence of Jesus is to be found in the witness of His forerunner, John the Baptist. This man was miraculously born, even as the One whose way he came to prepare, seeing his mother, Elisabeth, was very aged when she conceived her illustrious son (Luke 1:7, 13). From his birth, John was filled with the Holy Spirit, and by the same Spirit upheld the truth that Jesus lived before He was born in Bethlehem. Thus, when the forerunner came to baptize Jesus there was the same justification of Him as the One who had come from God, having dwelt in His bosom throughout the dateless past (John 1:18). Thus, three times over we find John declaring: "He that cometh after me is preferred before me: *for he was before me*" (John 1:15, 27, 30).

Then when John had baptized Jesus there was the same justification of Him, as the One who came as the Son in whom God was well-pleased. John saw the Holy Spirit descending from heaven, resting upon Jesus "like a dove" (John 1:32–34). By this symbol, both the Spirit and John vindicated that "that holy thing" born of Mary had lived a life of purity and peace throughout those thirty sinless, silent years in Nazareth. We have only one glimpse of His perfect character during this period in which Jesus grew to manhood, namely, the episode in the synagogue when He was only twelve years of age. His reply, then, to His agitated parents was most significant seeing it revealed the tenor of those hidden years, "Wist ye not that I must be about my Father's business?" (Luke 2:49).

The dove was also the emblem of the harmlessness and purity so characteristic of His brief but dynamic ministry of three years, a picture of the peace He had come to provide for a restless, sinning world. No wonder John "bare record that this is the Son of God" (John 1:34) and God Himself declared, "Thou art my beloved Son; in thee I am well pleased" (Luke 3:22). What a wonderful dual justification of the One who could say, "I do always those things that please Him (My Father)" (John 8:29), a confession inspiring many of His listeners to believe in Him.

We would have thought that such a well authenticated Person should have had the veneration, adoration, praise, and acceptance of all mankind. But no! In His humble home at Nazareth before He faced the world, He was misunderstood by those around Him. He was a stranger unto His brethren, and an alien to His mother's children (Ps. 69:8), and also something of an enigma to His mother and foster father, Joseph (Luke 2:48–51). Then when He came to discharge a heaven-given task, He endured three years of rejection, hatred, and humiliation from the religious leaders, as well as the animosity of hell. As Mary's Son, He did not occasion universal pleasure, but He had His Father's benediction and nothing else mattered.

Denouncing cities that had spurned Him and His message, predicting that they would be cast down to hell, and conscious that serpents and scorpions were combined to hurt Him, "In that hour Jesus rejoiced in spirit" (Luke 10:21). Weymouth translates the passage, "He was filled by the Holy Spirit with rapturous joy." Another rendering reads, "He was thrilled with joy at that hour in the Holy Spirit." Thus, the Spirit was not only His justifier, but also the source of our Lord's joy, enabling Him to triumph over His circumstances and to glory even in His tribulations. Anointed with the oil of gladness, He possessed an inward peace and tranquillity independent of all outward experiences and happenings (Heb. 1:9).

In all this Jesus left us an example that we should follow in His steps. As His followers we should know what it is to be dead to self-vindication, awaiting at all times the Spirit's justification, which, sooner or later, is given, much to the confusion of those who misjudge us. There is a difference between reputation and character. *Reputation* is what others think and say about us—*character* is what we actually are. Jesus cared not about His reputation, but flung it to the winds, making Himself of *no reputation* (Phil. 2:7). As to His character, it was perfect, for even Pilate confessed "I find no fault in this man." D.L. Moody used to say that "character is what a man is in the dark." If in our hidden heart, God is fully and obediently acknowledged and the Spirit of Joy is in possession of our being, then as the old rhyme puts it, sticks and stones may break our bones but names can never hurt us.

Although, in spite of those who did not believe in Jesus, the Holy Spirit could say *Amen* to all His claims to divine sonship, yet Peter reminds us that "the Spirit of Christ . . . testified beforehand the sufferings of Christ," and also of the vindicating glory that should follow (1 Peter 1:11; 2 Peter 1:21). The Spirit knew that this Man who received sinners, and ate and drank with them, would experience weariness, need of sleep, hunger, thirst, pain, soul trouble, agony of mind and body, tears, sorrow, shame, contempt, scourging, physical torture, and death. The Divine Vindicator also knew that amid all the trials and sufferings of this much-tried Man, He would declare the possession of a heart at peace with God, and assure His followers who would follow His steps in suffering, "Peace I leave with you, my peace I give unto you" (John 14:27).

The most outstanding, wonderful, and triumphant evidence of the Spirit's justification of the life, work and death of Jesus, however, was the Resurrection (Rom. 8:11). As "the spirit of holiness" (Rom. 1:4), He not only justified the claims of Jesus to deity, He often referred to it in the days of His humiliation, but also amply vindicated His sinlessness and His willingness to bear all suffering without retaliation. "When he was reviled, he reviled not again; when he suffered, he threatened not" (1 Peter 2:23). The marvel of the Gospel is that by His stripes we are healed (1 Peter 2:24). This is the divine example we are to emulate (1 Peter 3:9, 14, 17).

The New Testament affirms that the Holy Spirit was "the efficient cause" of our Lord's victory over the grave. "Put to death in the flesh, but quickened by the Spirit" (1 Peter 3:18). As the Spirit of Life, He made possible the conception of Jesus, and also the resurrection of Jesus. As in the virgin womb of Mary, the Spirit fashioned the physical body of Jesus, so in the virgin tomb of Joseph, He fashioned the glorified body of Jesus. The Roman authorities fixed their official seal on the outside of the tomb, affirming that Jesus would not rise again. But God has His seal—the Holy Spirit—within the tomb as evidence that He would rise again, and not see corruption (Ps. 16:1).

Thus, the Power giving the prenatal life and bringing it to birth was the same One who quickened our Lord's dead body and brought Him forth as the first begotten of the dead. The Spirit not only gave life to a corpse, but reunited the human spirit to its proper dwelling, not as a mere tenement, but as a home, insusceptible of further death. What a glorious vindication this was of all the previous claims of Jesus! Ellicott's *Commentary* says:

It was by His resurrection from the dead that Christ's lofty claims to the Godhead were justified. His own assertions respecting Himself were triumphantly vindicated . . . In the power of the Spirit, He did take His life which He had laid down, did reunite His soul unto His body for which He separated it when He gave up the ghost, and so did quicken and revive Himself, and thus publicly proclaimed His divine nature, His awful dignity.[1]

Up from the grave He arose,
With a mighty triumph o'er His foes:
He arose a Victor from the dark domain,
And He lives for ever with His saints to reign!
He arose! He arose!
Hallelujah! Christ arose.[2]

---

[1] Ellicott, *Commentary.*
[2] Robert Lowry, "Christ Arose"; from *The Great Hymns* (Tabernacle Publishing Co.) 71.

4

HIS REVELATION

Seen of Angels (1 Tim. 3:16)

Way's translation of the phrase, "seen of angels" reads, "Was an Object of open vision to angels." Much as we may desire to dwell upon a full coverage of the origin, nature, and ministry of Angels, our attention must be focused upon Paul's brief sentence, "*seen of angels,*" in its relation to the context, namely, the revelation of God in a human form. That this "open vision" of the angels is definitely associated with the period covering Christ's descent from heaven to become *Man*, till His ascent to heaven as the glorified Man, is borne out by their unique and specific ministry while He was among men, and also by what He taught regarding the office of angels.

Whether the angelic host beheld Jesus in the dateless past, when He shared the presence of the Father, or veiled their faces in the blazing glory of their presence, we do not know. What is evident is that they unceasingly worshipped and adored Him as the Creator and Lord and as the express Image of the Father. When, however, the Son of God became God manifest in flesh—a Babe born of a woman—this was the marvel that riveted their gaze and caused their wonder and praise to rise to their greatest height. "When he bringeth in the first begotten into the world, he saith, And let all the angels of God worship Him" (Heb. 1:6), and worship Him they did, as we shall presently indicate, with a greater intensity than in the past Eternity when He dwelt in the bosom of the Father.

When Isaiah came to record his sublime vision he says that he beheld how the angels veiled their faces in adoring worship of Him who was their Creator, and heard them cry to one another, "Holy, holy, holy, is the Lord of Hosts" (Isa. 6:3). But when John came to reveal the angelic worship of Jesus after His return as the Lamb who had taken away the sin of the world, he wrote of the uncountable number of angels whose worship and praise knew no bounds as they dwelt on their dominant theme, "Worthy is the Lamb that was slain" (Rev. 5:12; see Phil. 2:9–11). Those joyful angels realized that as the result of the Word being made flesh and tabernacling among men, and ultimately dying for their redemption, He was "much better" than they, and through His life and sacrifice had "obtained a more excellent name then they" (Heb. 1:4).

The question for our hearts is, if the delight and worship of angels are so intense, seeing that we owe Jesus more than angels do, should not our adoration equal or exceed that of these ministers of His will? Are we not bound to Him by ties of which they know nothing, for was it not for them that He endured agony and bloody sweat, and died upon the cross? Further, it is *our* nature, and not the nature of angels, that Jesus wears for ever in heaven. Therefore our love to Him ought to be stronger; our reverence for Him deeper; our devotion to him more perfect. Because He bought us at a price at which angels were not purchased, should He not find us lost in adoration, praise and worship?

It may prove to be a fitting introduction to our meditation on how the angels saw and served the Lord Jesus while He was among men as the Son of Man, to consider the intriguing question as to the precise occasion when the angelic host came to understand the full significance of their Creator's incarnation. Peter, in his reference to the prophets who "inquired and searched diligently" the revelation of divine grace, and who was inspired by the Spirit to testify *beforehand* "the sufferings of Christ, and the glory that should follow," goes on to say that these were truths "which the angels desire to look into" (1 Peter 1:10–12). In His parable of the fig tree, Jesus affirmed that at the time He spoke *angels,* like men below, knew not the day nor hour of His coming judgment upon the godless earth (Matt. 24:36).

The attitude Peter ascribes to angels implies a distinct apprehension of the wonder and purpose of the Incarnation, and is reminiscent of the cherubim and seraphim bending over the Mercy Seat in the

Tabernacle of old. At each end of the Mercy Seat, beaten out of pure gold, was carved a winged cherub with the faces of the two cherubim turned one to another, and placed in an attitude or worship over the ark, as if with an earnest desire to look into the mysteries hidden under the golden lid. This same gaze is what Peter emphasizes in his phrase, "to look," which literally means "to bend aside to see," a sense used of those "standing at the side of the cave so as not to get in their own light, and stooping sideways to peer in." The phrase implies, "a strained attention to something which caught your eye somewhat out of your usual line of sight."

Being *angels*, they were present before time when one of their leaders in the angelic hierarchy, Lucifer, yielding to pride and ambition, sought to be exalted as a member of the Godhead, and along with those angels who rebelled with him, was expelled from heaven (Isa. 14:12–17; see Ezek. 28:12–15). The remaining obedient angels doubtless heard the first pronouncement of the coming of the Son of God to earth to destroy the works of the devil and his angels, and they were gratified that the seed of the woman would bruise the serpent's head (Gen. 3:15). A knowledge, then, was theirs of Satan's expulsion from the courts above, and of the plan of redemption, which was to involve the death of God's beloved Son.

Living in the light of the divine throne, they gathered knowledge from the fountainhead, and so learned all about God's holiness in the expulsion of their fallen companions from heaven, and of the terrible judgment the devil and his angels would ultimately suffer as the result of Jesus coming in the fullness of time, as One born of a Woman. However, the secret these inquiring angels sought to probe was *how* and *when* His incarnation would be accomplished. As the wisdom of God was bound up with the means He was to employ for the Word to be made flesh, the exact method and moment of such a transformation was one of the things into which those holy angels wanted a deeper insight.

A further thought is that although those angels desired to look into the sufferings of Christ and the glory o follow (John 17:22–24), they knew that they would have no share in same: that He was to die on our behalf, not theirs: they could never experience "the fellowship of his sufferings" and know "the power of his resurrection." Yet although such participation can never be theirs, these heaven-sent messengers ever rejoice over all Jesus accomplished for the vindication of God's holiness, and for the deliverance of sinners from the tyranny of sin (Rev. 12:7–12; see 5:11, 12; 7:11–17; 14:6, 7). Let us now seek to summarize the mention and ministry of angels in the Four Gospels, covering as they did the life and labor of the preexistent One who was manifested in human form.

The Forerunner of Jesus

The first reference to angels in Luke is found in the foretelling by "an angel of the Lord," ((Luke 1:11) of the coming of John the Baptist to prepare the way for the appearance of the long-promised Messiah. Zacharias and Elisabeth were persons of singular piety, being "righteous before God" and practiced in the spiritual loveliness, for both "walked in all the commandments and ordinances of the Lord blameless" (Luke 1:6). Both were also "well stricken in years" (Luke 1:7). Tradition has it that Elisabeth was eighty-nine years of age and Zacharias, a few years older than his wife.

While Zacharias was engaged in his sacred duty at the altar, a celestial messenger stood near. Seeing him, Zacharias was afraid. The majestic stranger quickly announced his mission, however: "Fear not, Zacharias: for thy prayer is heard; and thy wife Elisabeth shall bear thee a son, and thou shalt call his name *John*" (Luke 1:13). Venturing a reply, the priest pointed out the natural impossibility of such an unexpected promise, seeing his wife was incapable of bearing a child because of her advanced age. Asking for a sign from the angel that the birth of a son would be a reality, he received a most unexpected one, namely, dumbness. On the other hand Elisabeth believed the gracious word of the Lord the angel had announced. She conceived, and at the appointed time had her reproach among men as a childless wife taken away. Thus, like Isaac who was born to Abraham and Sarah when they were very old (Gen. 17:7–23; 18:2–14; 21:5), John also was miraculously conceived, just as the One whose way he had come to prepare would be. Both Elisabeth and Mary learn that "with God nothing shall be impossible" (Luke 1:37).

With the birth of John, the speech of his righteous father was restored. Filled with the Holy Spirit, he announced of his son, who was filled with the same spirit from his birth:

> Thou, child, shalt be called the prophet of the Highest: for thou shalt go before the face of the Lord to prepare his ways; to give knowledge of salvation unto his people by the remission of their sins, through the tender mercy of our God; whereby the dayspring from on high hath visited us, to give light to them that sit in darkness, and in the shadow of death to guide our feet in the way of peace (Luke 1:76–79).

As for John himself, when the time came for his showing unto Israel, this extraordinary child, now a young man commissioned by the Spirit of God, preached that he was only a voice crying in the wilderness calling upon the people that although he baptized the repentant in water, One would soon come who would baptize with the Holy Spirit and fire; and that this One being mightier than he was, he was not worthy to unloose the latchet of His shoes (Luke 3:1–20). His was the sacred privilege of baptizing Jesus in Jordan and also of being the first martyr for declaring the mission of the Savior whose way he prepared. As for Jesus Himself, He declared that "Among them that are born of woman there hath not arisen a greater than John the Baptist" (Matt. 11:11).

The first appearance of Gabriel, the only heavenly messenger to be named in the Gospels, then, was of the utmost significance, for he not only determined the name Zacharias and Elisabeth should call their illustrious son, but he announced that the Babe (to be shortly born after John) was the Lord God of the children of Israel—God manifest in flesh for their salvation (Luke 1:69). Thus, the early preparation for the coming of the God-Man so clearly foretold by Gabriel, angelic spokesman for God, indicated divine fidelity and grace.

The Mother of Jesus

Devout hearts preparing to meditate upon the unique ministry of angels in connection with the birth of our beloved Savior realize the necessity of approaching such a solemn theme in "reverence and godly fear," for "the place whereon [they stand] is holy ground" (Exod. 3:5). Virginity of heart is necessary if our finite mind is to grasp the great mystery of our Christian faith, namely, Christ's miraculous birth by the Virgin Mary. The fact that He, by His birth, became "Emmanuel . . . *God with us*" (Matt. 1:23) involving as it did the incarnation of deity, the personal union of the Godhead with a human infant, is far above the comprehension of the loftiest intellect of man, and perhaps even the angels themselves. What a comforting truth this is to carry with us through the day, that God is with us. God in our bodily form is our sole consolation. Jesus came with the nature of His Father, hence His ability to be our everyday Friend, calming our fears, sympathizing with us in our sorrows. He also has our nature, hence His suitability to meet our needs and cause all things to work together for our good. Jesus is God with us—in us—for us! So, take courage, the ear of thy Emmanuel is ever open, the heart of thy Emmanuel is ever tender, the arm of thy Emmanuel is ever strong. We must clearly understand that there was a man of two natures, the divine and human, in the Person of our Lord Jesus Christ. It is a point of the deepest importance. We should settle it firmly in our minds, that our Savior is perfect man as well as perfect God. The name Emmanuel takes in the whole mystery.

Jesus was to come of the seed of the woman, not of man, which was fulfilled when He was conceived of the Holy Spirit and born of the *Virgin* Mary. Thus, by the manner of conception, the holiness of His nature was secured and His fitness to be the Savior of a sinful world assured to all mankind. *Man* only is the product of natural generation; but "the man Christ Jesus," born of the Virgin was "that holy thing" (Luke 1:35), the Son of God—composed of a pure and unpolluted humanity in the temple of deity.

Says Malcolm Muggeridge, "To a twentieth-century mind the notion of a virgin birth is intrinsically and preposterously inconceivable. If a woman claims—such claims are made from time to time—to have become pregnant without sexual intercourse, no one believes her. Yet for centuries millions upon millions of people never doubted that Mary had begotten Jesus without the participation of a husband or lover. Nor was such a belief limited to the simple and unlettered; the most profound and most erudite minds, the greatest artists and craftsmen, found no difficulty in accepting the Virgin Birth as an incontestable fact—for instance, Pascal, who in the versatility of his gifts and the originality of his insights was regarded as the Aristotle of his time."

Are we, then, to suppose that our forebears who believed implicitly in the virgin birth were gullible fools?

Of the royal house of David, Mary, herself although young, was one of the many who "were looking for redemption in Israel" (Luke 2:38). But what a soul-moving revelation and experience it must have been when she learned from the angel Gabriel that *she* was to be the mother of the glorious Redeemer, when honored by this heavenly visitant, who addressed her by her proper name. Calmed by the beaming benevolence of Gabriel, Mary spoke to him with unaffected modesty, holy meekness, and rational piety, as the seraphic messenger satisfied her inquiries and removed all her scruples.

> Then said Mary to the angel, How shall this be, seeing I know not a man? And the angel answered and said unto her, The Holy Ghost shall come upon thee, and the power of the Highest shall overshadow thee: therefore also that holy thing which shall be born of thee, shall be called the Son of God" (Luke 1:34, 35).

Gabriel not only uttered her name as he announced the birth of her Son, but he told Mary by what name she should call Him: "Thou . . . shalt call his name *Jesus*" (Luke 1:31). Does this not prove how intimately the angels, as ministering spirits, are with all the circumstances of the people of God? Without doubt, Jesus is the sweetest name on mortal tongue and is—

> That name I fondly love to hear,
> It never fails my heart to cheer,
> Its music dries a falling tear;
> Exalt the name of Jesus.

It is most appropriate that Luke should be chosen to record the delicate, intimate aspect of the conception and birth of Jesus, for as "the beloved physician" (Col. 4:14) and a believer, he was well qualified to set forth those things eyewitnesses surely believed (Luke 1:1–4). In his *Contemplations* written over a century ago Bishop Hall said:

The Spirit of God was never so accurate in any description as that which concerns the Incarnation of God. It was fit that no circumstance should be omitted in that story, whereon the faith and salvation of the world dependeth. We cannot so much as doubt of this truth, and be saved. No; not the number of the month, nor the name of the angel, is concealed. Every particle imports not more certainty, than excellence—The Messenger is an angel. A man was too mean to carry the news of the conception of God. Never any business was conceived in heaven, that did so much concern the earth, as the conception of God in the womb of the earth. No less than an archangel was worthy to bear this tiding; and never any angel received a greater honor, than of this message.

We might add that never a man received a greater honor than Luke did when he was guided by the Spirit to write out in order all that the celestial messenger had declared to Zacharias, Elisabeth, Mary, and Joseph. This is why Luke's *Gospel* presents Jesus as the human-divine One, just as John reveals Him as the divine-human One. Jesus as "The Son of God" who became "The Son of Man" is the keynote of Luke's wonderful record.

It may be fitting at this point to emphasize that among the multitudes of the angelic army around the throne of God, only two of the unfallen angels are specifically named—Michael and Gabriel—both of whom were among the first rank of angels and were given the most important missions on earth to fulfill.

A comparison of the two is interesting. *Michael,* meaning "who is like unto God," has a name suggesting self-oblation, self-obliteration. He never gloried in himself. He would not rebuke the devil, but he left him to the Lord (Jude 9). *The Book of Enoch* extols his meekness, calling him, "the merciful, the patient, the holy Michael." He is found connected with many events in the history of Moses (Exod. 2:12; Deut. 34:6), and with appearances to Daniel as "one of the chief princes" (Dan. 10:13, 21; 12:1). He is also mentioned twice in the New Testament (Jude 9; Rev. 12:7).

Gabriel, meaning "the strength, or hero, of God," appears fewer times than his fellow archangel. He had two missions to Daniel (8:15; 9:21) and then his missions to Zacharias and Mary. His was the greatest privilege any angel ever had, seeing he was chosen to proclaim the birth of Jesus.

A comparison of these holy two reveals Michael to be the champion who fought the battles of faith, and who was ever on the side of his God (2 Kings 6:17). He it was who overcame the evil, satanic prince of Persia, and his great celestial and militant host are the seraphs who warred against the devil and his angels.

As for Gabriel, he is not referred to as having contact with the devil. Someone has said, "There is in his manifestation a simplicity and absence of terror corresponding to his character as comforter." He is the angel who wrote down divine decrees, the angelic prophet, interpreter of the prophetic Word, and revealer of the purposes of God. He was sent to man in the form of a man before God sent His Son to take human form.

Further, it may have been that by the announcement of Gabriel to Mary the inquiring angels received the *how, when,* and *where* of the promised Messiah's birth. As we have already indicated, the angelic host desired to peer into these holy things. The broad truth that their Creator was to become a Child was known to them from the fall of Satan and God's promise of a Deliverer, but *how* the miracle was to happen was the mystery solved for them when their leader declared that He would be conceived of the Holy Spirit and born of the Virgin Mary. What rapture must have been theirs when they beheld the union of Deity and Humanity in a Babe.

If God chose to become incarnate as Jesus, then His birth, whatever marvels may have accompanied it, must have had the same characteristics as any other; just as, on the Cross, the suffering of the man into whom the Bethlehem child grew must have been of the same nature as that of the two delinquents crucified beside Him. Otherwise, Jesus' humanity would have been a fraud; in which case, His divinity would have been fraudulent, too. The perfection of Jesus' divinity was expressed in the perfection of His humanity, and vice versa. He was God because He was so sublimely a man, and Man because, in all His sayings and doings, in the grace of His person and words, in the love and compassion that shone out of Him, He walked so closely with God. As Man alone, Jesus could not have saved us; as God alone, He would not; Incarnate, He could and did.

We must return to Mary herself, however. Deeply affected by the appearance and announcement of Gabriel, and accepting his message about her cousin Elisabeth, who was old enough to be her mother, Mary was anxious to ascertain the truth of the miraculous event she expected. How Elisabeth must have been overwhelmed as her youthful, virgin cousin recounted the marvelous communication of Gabriel! To quote Bishop Hall again:

> Only the meeting of saints in Heaven can parallel the meeting of these two cousins; the two wonders of the world are met under one roof and congratulate their mutual happiness.

The remarkable Spirit-inspired benediction of Elisabeth was "a magnificent canticle in which the strain of Hannah's ancient song, in like circumstances is caught up, and just slightly modified and sub-limed." What a most apt expression of devout praise it was, revealing Mary's humility, faith and privilege! What deep joy must have been hers as her longed-for babe leaped in her womb while in Mary's presence: "a sympathetic emotion of the unconscious babe, at the presence of Mary the mother of his Lord." What a remarkable phrase Elisabeth used in her sincere, heartfelt congratulation: "Whence is this to me, that the mother of my Lord should come to me?" (Luke 1:43). Jamieson's *Commentary* quotes Olshausen as saying:

> Turn this as we will, we shall never be able to see the propriety of calling an unborn child—*Lord*—but by supposing Elisabeth, like the prophets of old, enlightened to perceive the Messiah's *Divine nature.* "The mother of *my Lord*"—but not *my lady.* See Luke 22:42; John 20:28.[1]

As for Mary, in her *Magnificat*, influenced with the same heavenly inspiration as her aged cousin, she burst forth in expressions of exulting joy which revealed her richly furnished and devout mind (Luke

---

[1] Jamieson, et. al., *Commentary,* 97

1:46–55). The verse that stands out in her tribute to Him who had done great things for her is the one in which she confesses that the Babe she was to bear would be *her* Savior, as well as the Savior of the world. "My soul doth magnify the Lord, and my spirit hath rejoiced in God *my* Saviour" (Luke 1:46, 47). The terms, *my soul—my spirit*, implies "all that is within me" (Ps. 103:1). An immaculate life was evidently hers, otherwise God would not have chosen her—a virgin—to be a mother. Yet she voided her need of the salvation her Son would provide: and generations have called her blessed for such a confession.

In conclusion, we turn to Joseph, who, discovering Mary's pregnant condition, was overwhelmed. Dreading the shame that must unavoidably cover one who had been so dear to him, he sought direction in his perplexity from God, for he knew that in cases of infidelity, the law of God required divorcement, denouncing, a terrible punishment of death by stoning (Deut. 22:23, 24). Graciously God answered Joseph's plea through the ministry of an angel (Matt. 1:18–25). Through the same angelic agency Joseph was instructed to flee into Egypt, and then, at a safe time return (Matt. 2:13–15, 19, 20). It does not appear as if Mary had made known to Joseph her peculiar condition. Probably she left her cause and reputation to her covenant God, and the angelic visit Joseph received rewarded her confidence and faith by removing every vestige of doubt from his upright and candid mind, in relation to the virtue of his espoused wife. Timpson, in his incomparable study, *The Angels of God* (a remarkable volume, many thoughts of which I have adapted), ends his chapter on *Virgin Mary* with his unique tribute to Joseph:

> Mary's unspotted purity being thus established by the special testimony of Heaven—in perfect accordance with the statement which must have been made by Mary herself, as to the visit of the angel Gabriel—the servant of God made no hesitation in obeying the Divine command, following the dictates of his own benevolent heart. "Then Joseph, being raised up from sleep, did as the angel of the Lord had bidden him, and took unto him his wife" (Matt. 1:24).

> While we admire the merciful condescension of God toward the Virgin Mary, in the mission of the angel Gabriel, we behold in Joseph a fine example of gentleness and prudence. He was careful

to avoid any precipitate steps; and in the critical moments of his anxious deliberation, God, who knew his uprightness and single-ness of heart, graciously interposed to guide and determine his resolutions. Joseph's decision, in taking Mary to his own home, when satisfied by the assurance of the angel of the Lord, was worthy of his reputation for piety, and it affords to us an instruc-tive pattern of prompt obedience, whenever our duty may call us to glorify our God and Saviour.[2]

The Birth of Jesus

What a jubilant day it was for the angelic hierarchy of heaven when they gazed upon the face of the newborn King! When "the angel," probably Gabriel, made his announcement to the pious, poor shep-herds, the multitude of the heavenly host, accompanying the angels, became happy songsters and formed themselves into a hallelujah chorus to praise God. The birth of the Babe was "good tidings of great joy" not only "to all people," but also to the angelic legions as they beheld human nature so highly exalted: "that God was man, and man was God. Seeing God so humbled, and man so changed, and so full of charity, that God stooped to the condition of man, and man was inflamed beyond the love of seraphim, and was made more knowing than cherubims, more established than thrones, more happy than the order of angels."[3]

Sing, though they did, as angels alone can sing, the Song of Re-demption was one they could not join in (Heb. 2:16).

A song which even angels
Shall never never sing:
They know not Christ as Saviour,
But worship Him as King.

Happy to surround the throne of God, they will never be privileged as saints to share His throne (Rev. 3:21; 5:11). Let us try to appreciate,

---

[2] Timpson, *Angels*, 392.
[3] Ibid., 398.

however, the happy welcome with which the angels introduced Jesus to a sinful and sinning world.

The first impressive feature of the birth-narratives is the marked differences apparent in this account of this greatest event in world history. Think of the comparison between the dazzling glory of the Lord which usually encompassed heavenly visions and visitations (the angelic revelation of the greatest tiding ever published abroad), the seraphic serenaders proclaiming the shortest, greatest sermon ever preached, and then joining with the utmost insignificant participants of earth! What honored company did Gabriel address. Was it to the proud Roman, Herod, "the king of the Jews," "the master of the World," and to his haughty nobles living in luxurious significance in their stately mansions, or did the blessed angel hasten to the priests and Levites guarding the sacred fires in the temple?

The Babe the angels praised came not to be King; He was *born* a King, but no worldly pomp awaited the approach of this heavenly King. No flourish of trumpets heralded the event. No palace was built to receive Him. No purple robes were ready for His adornment. The beauty of this greatest story ever told is that the poor but pious shepherds who, as they watched their flocks at night (doubtless meditating upon the ancient Scripture prophesying that the Messiah would come as the *Good Shepherd*) were the first to receive the good tidings Gabriel had brought from heaven. These shepherds along with other devout Jews waited for the redemption of Israel and their reward came when the darkness of one night was filled with splendor, and their night was turned to day—symbolic of the spiritual mission of Him who had come as the Light of the World. But if the Shepherds were the first to receive news of His birth and also the first to see Jesus, the sages from afar had the *next* sight of the new-born King. It is "even so, still simplicity first, science next, finds its way to Christ." As Keble expresses it:

> In quiet ever and in shade
> Shepherds and Sage may find—
> They who have bowed themselves untaught to Nature's sway,
> And they, who follow Truth along her star-paved way.

The sign given the devout and lowly Shepherds that the divine announcement was authentic was that the Babe would be found in a manger when they went to Bethlehem to "see this thing which is come to pass, which the Lord hath made known unto us" (Luke 2:15). Coming from the spaciousness and splendor of the Father's house, with its many mansions, the Babe found no royal nursery with a beautifully prepared crib to receive Him, although a winged seraph from the court of heaven had been commissioned to announce His birth. No palace or noble mansion was open to welcome Joseph and Mary, even though they were of a royal family, and signally honored by the King Eternal. Being poor they were not financially able to procure desirable accommodation, not even within the small wayside inn, so that Mary could have the privacy her delicate condition required.

John reminds us that Jesus came unto His own, but that they received Him not (1:11). Well, He certainly came to His own world, which He created, but there was no room even in the modest inn for Him, and so His godly mother was forced to endure the humiliating necessity of bringing forth her firstborn in a stable. For His cradle, He had a manger, or crib or stall, in which food for animals was placed. What a humiliation for both mother and Babe—especially for the Babe who came as the "Lord of Glory" manifest in flesh. Keble also has the stanza on this grim experience:

Wrapt in His swaddling-bands,
And in His manger laid,
The hope and glory of all lands
Is come to the world's aid.
No peaceful home upon His cradle smiled,
Guests rudely went and came where slept
the royal Child.

God, however, had sent His own illustrious visitors to pay court to Him who was to say to Pilate, as He came to die, "Thou sayest that I am a king. To this end was I born, and for this cause came I into the world" (John 18:37). The contrast between the glorious descriptions given Him at His birth, and the conditions in which He would be found, is overpowering. He, whose goings have been from of old, from everlasting to everlasting, would be seen as a Babe in the crib of oxen; He whom the heaven of heavens could not contain would be discovered "wrapt in swaddling clothes"—a mystery angels desired to see. Paul seems to have had these amazing contrasts in mind when he wrote, "Though he was rich, yet for your sakes he became poor, that ye through his poverty might be rich" (2 Cor. 8:9).

Rich! As the preexistent One, the Lord of glory, and of angels, this beloved Son dwelt in the bosom of the Father, became *poor*, so very poor, for He came as the Son of another man's spouse, born in another man's abode, dined at another man's table, slept in another man's boat, rode on another man's ass, and was buried in another man's grave. Truly He sounded the depths of humiliation for our sakes!

Through His poverty we might be rich. Yes, enriched beyond measure, with riches of His grace and mercy here and now, and in the life to come, the riches of glory as our eternal inheritance.

A courier is described by the dictionary as "a messenger," and this is how Gabriel functioned when he appeared to the shepherds overawed and frightened by the glory of the Lord enveloping them. "Fear not," said the courier, who was heaven's messenger to the faithful shepherds, and then there followed the message heaven commissioned him to deliver: "Behold, I bring you good tidings of great joy, which shall be to all people" (Luke 2:11). Thus the angel declared the universality of the gospel. The qualifying terms *good* and *great joy* indicate the nature of the gospel itself. Salvation for a lost world was surely the greatest, most joyous news mankind has ever received. Here, then, is the news:

> By Thee the joyful news
> Of my salvation came;
> The joyful news of sin forgiven,
> Of Hell subdued, and peace
> with Heaven.

The Time of His Birth—"This Day"

Traditionally, we celebrate December 25 as the natal day of Jesus. Many Bible scholars, however, feel that His birthday was a few days later, early in January. While we may never know the exact moment of

His incarnation, the fact that matters is that He was born to give man second birth. The day of which Gabriel spoke was *the* day that the Word was *made flesh.*

The Place of His Birth—"The City of David"

The inspired prediction required that the Messiah should be born in Bethlehem, as the advent song of Micah made clear. "Thou, Bethlehem Ephratah, though thou be little among the thousands of Judah, yet out of thee shall he come forth unto me, that is to be ruler in Israel; whose goings forth have been of old, from everlasting" (5:2). So prophecy directed Israel where to look for Him, and their faith accordingly expected Him. Before Christ was born the whole Sanhedrin designated Bethlehem as the birthplace of the expected Messiah (Matt. 2:4–6).

But somehow little attention has been given to God's overruling providence as seen in Jesus coming of the right *line*—the House of David; at the right *place*—the city of David. Without these historic moorings of our faith substantial Christianity would be lost. Gabriel's visitation to Mary took him to Nazareth, where this saint dwelt, but Gabriel's appearance to the shepherds to announce the birth of Him who was conceived by the Spirit in Nazareth found him in Bethlehem some one hundred miles from Nazareth.

While Joseph and Mary doubtless knew of Micah's prophecy about Bethlehem being the birthplace of Jesus, they remained in their usual abode in Nazareth. How, then, did the unexpected, slow, and arduous journey (particularly for Mary) come about? Behind such we see how God can make the most unlikely events subservient to the accomplishment of His designs, as Timpson suggests in his unique work on *Angels*:

> The vanity of a heathen monarch, in a distant country, was overruled to bring about the completion of the Divine purposes: for Augustus Caesar, the Roman Emperor, is allowed to "set his unwieldy empire in motion, from the Baltic to the Atlantic, and from Britain, or Gaul, to the extremity of Egypt and Syria" for this purpose. He issued, therefore, an edict for a census of all his subjects to be made; and the enrollment of the whole population

of Canaan required that the inhabitants of Judah, though living in distant towns, should register themselves in the places of their original family inheritances, Luke 2:1–4. Hence Joseph and Mary, at the momentous period, being of the royal "house and lineage," though greatly reduced in circumstances, repaired to Bethlehem, the city of David, for the necessary registration. Infinite wisdom arranged the whole plan for the advent of the great Messiah."[4]

The Given Names at His Birth

Mary was spared the problem of a typical mother having to choose the most fitting name for her child, not knowing what sex her baby would be.

But Mary knew her Babe would be a Son. His name not only for life but for eternity was chosen by heaven. "His name was called Jesus, which was so named of the angel before he was conceived in the womb" (Luke 2:21). Then there are the three names the angel announced: namely, *Saviour—Christ—Lord* (Luke 2:11). What marvelous, imperishable names, or titles, these are!

1. Saviour!

The angelic bearer of this God-given name did not say to the shepherds, "One who *shall be a saviour*," but "born a saviour," implying He was such *before* he was born. "My people . . . he was their Saviour" (Isa. 63:8). According to His own teaching, Jesus came to "seek and save the lost." He did not come, as some would claim, to be a great social reformer, a great teacher, a great philanthropist, and great martyr who died for truth in which He believed. In a way, He was all these, but the Scripture looks at Jesus only from the standpoint of the World's Redeemer, who was born and died to save sinners (see 1 Cor. 15:3).

2. Christ-Lord

The angel paired these names together, saying, "*Who is Christ the Lord!*" Dean Alford said of this magnificent appellation, "This is the

---

[4]Timpson, *Angels*, 394–95.

only place where these words come together: and I see no way of understanding this *Lord*, but as corresponding to the Hebrew *Jehovah*." Aged Simeon was assured by the Holy Spirit that he would not die until he had seen "the Lord's Christ" (Luke 2:26). What convincing proof of His dual nature, of "*God* manifest in *flesh*," in "A babe lying in a manger," and "Christ the Lord"!

The Angelic Choir

How the midnight air must have vibrated as the singing of the heavenly choristers suddenly burst upon the ears of the already awestruck shepherds! Did they not listen to the greatest song ever given to earth at night (Luke 2:13–14)? Never before or since has the world been privileged to hear a massed choir of such a vast number as this one which existed to praise God and which had only a few poor shepherds as an audience. Says Paul, as "God manifest in flesh," Jesus was "seen of angels," and what a force it must have given to their singing as they beheld their Creator and Lord as a Babe wrapped in swaddling clothes. Those angelic songsters were like "an *army* celebrating *peace*," says Bengal. Of their singing, in which Gabriel must have joined, seeing the heavenly host had come to seal and celebrate the good and joyful tidings he had just brought, one wrote, "The heavenly host transferring the occupation of their exalted station to this poor earth, who so seldom resounds with the pure praise of God, to let it be known how this event is regarded in *heaven* and should be regarded on *earth*."

Their Number

The term *multitude* raises the question of how many unfallen angels there are making up such "an army in heaven," which acts only according to God's will, and which were present at the birth of Jesus. When Jesus asked the leader of the devils, or demons, or fallen angels, what his name was, he replied, "My name is Legion; for we are many" (Luke 8:30). Mark states that the number of evil spirits possessing the maniac was about "two thousand" (5:13). All of these, expelled by Jesus from the man, entered swine nearby, but the pigs rather than be demon-possessed committed suicide by drowning.

As to the exact number of the unfallen angels Scripture is silent, only using language implying a vast contingent of them. John Milton, the blind poet, gave us the lines:

> Nor think—though men were none—
> That Heaven would want spectators, God want praise!
> Millions of spiritual creatures walk the earth.
> Unseen, both when we wake and when we sleep.
> All these with ceaseless praise His works behold
> Both day and night.

That angels are to be counted by myriads throughout the illimitable universe of God is seen in the language used of them, as of the multitudinous stars (Deut.. 4:19; Job 38:7; Ps. 148:1–6; Isa. 24:21–23; 34:4). When Jacob returned to Padan-aram "the angels of God met him . . . and he called he name of the place *Mahanaim* (or two hosts or armies)" (Gen. 32:1, 2). Moses wrote of the innumerable company of angels as "the host of heaven" who were not to be worshipped (Deut. 17:3; see Joshua 5:14). The psalmist sang, "The chariots of God are twenty thousand, even thousands of angels" (Ps. 68:17; 89:6–8). Similar language is used by Micaiah and Elisha's servant (1 Kings 22:17; 2 Kings 6:17). As for Daniel, he speaks of "thousand thousands . . . ten thousand times ten thousand" of angels ministering unto God (Dan. 7:10).

When Jesus prevented Peter from defending Him against His foes, He spoke of "twelve legions" of angels of all ranks as being ready to rally to His aid, if He so wished (Matt. 26:53). A *legion* was the largest division of the Roman army, composed of 6,200 foot soldiers, and 300 horse soldiers. Thus *twelve legions* would represent well over 72,000. It is because of the impressive size of a legion that the term came to represent a large number in orderly combination, such as the "ten thousand times ten thousand, and thousands and thousands" surrounding the throne of God (Rev. 5:11). Such numbers are symbolic of a countless throng who—

Loud as from numbers without number, sweet
As from blest voices, uttering joy.

Hesiod, the most ancient of the uninspired writers, yet acknowledged the existence of angels, and wrote of their ministry to men on earth in these lines:

Aerial spirits, by great Jove designed,
To be on earth the guardians of mankind;
Invisible to mortal eyes they go,
And mark our actions, good or bad below;
Th' immortal spies with watchful care preside,
And thrice ten thousand round their charges glide.
They can reward with glory or with gold;
Such power Divine Permission bids them hold.

Their Oratoria

If those of earth, apart from the few humble folk who had received the revelation of the great mystery of godliness, were silent at the coming of the King, the skies were vocal with praise as heaven sent forth all its armies to escort the Eternal Son into our world, and pay homage to Him at the One worthy to receive royal honors. If, as the King Himself came to declare, "There is joy in the presence of the angels of God" (Luke 15:10) over the repentance of one sinner, then surely all heavenly principalities and powers must have been thrilled at the greatest event in human history, namely, the Incarnation of Him who was to bring many souls to glory. If, at the creation of the world, "the morning stars sang together, and all the sons of God shouted for joy" (Job 38:7), how could even one seraph be silent when the world was about to receive its predicted Redeemer? Why, the angelic choir sang a song of the Babe born in Bethlehem, such a cradle song as was never was sung of a monarch's son; for in those swaddling clothes was wrapped the grand mystery angels desired to see.

The anthem they sang in notes of triumphant gladness also ascended to heaven with the melody of thanksgiving to God. The angelic song soared to heaven, then stooped to earth, and concluded with men, as though it would forever echo in human hearts—which, of course, it has. A comment from the last century reminds us that at the very heart of this song, "Praise rises up to the glory of God; comes down again to proffer peace on earth; rests with good will on men. . . . Now is the glory of God manifested in making earth peaceful, by mercy and good will shown to sinful man!"

The substance of the song of the celestial choir, although expressed in only twelve words, is yet of great scope. It is in three brief, unforgettable parts, which we taken in order:

> Glory to God in the highest
> Peace on earth
> Good will toward men.

Glory to God in the Highest

This first note gives harmony to the remaining two lines, seeing it is the assurance of what will be accomplished through the redemptive work of Him, who, as a *Child* was *born*, and as a *Son* was *given*. If men fail to grasp that their "chief end is to glorify God, and to enjoy Him for ever," angels certainly made such a blessed end their main objective. Actually, the angels in their theme song affirmed that because Jesus was born the *Savior*, His work in saving sinners, defeating the devil, abolishing death, and making an end of sin, should give rise to a new revenue of glory to God. In *creation*, God's omnipotence, wisdom, and love were revealed; in *judgment*, with the swift vengeance that overtook the angels who sinned, His justice was manifested; in *redemption*, God displayed through the coming of the Redeemer His matchless grace, an attribute of the Godhead now fully displayed, and which the angels praised in their exaltation of divine glory.

Those holy, happy angels adored *divine wisdom* in the solution of the difficult problem of how the glory of a thrice-holy God and the salvation of guilty sinners could be harmonized—how one could be displayed as the other is maintained. Those seraphic singers also magnified *divine holiness* as they saw the Father pass the sword of judgment into the bosom of His only begotten, well-beloved Son, just born as the Sin-bearer. Those celestial, joyous hosts likewise praised *divine justice*, as they discovered that the Surety must die that sinners might live; that no general act of amnesty would pardon the guilty, but that God punished their sins in Jesus, His Son, who died "the just for the unjust, that he might bring us to God" (1 Peter 3:18). Those "sons of the morning" extolled *divine power* that was to be more preeminently illustrated in the salvation of the lost than it could have been in their destruction, and more abundantly illustrated in redemption than creation.

Peace on Earth

How true it is that there would be no real peace on earth except it come in a way honourable to God and consistent with His divine glory! The original, blessed communion with God was forfeited by Adam through disobedience, and so the two could no longer walk together, for they were not agreed. How, then, was the breach to be healed? Certainly not by anything the estranged sinner could do, who left to himself must perish. The proverb has it, "Man's extremity is God's opportunity," and He maintained His character as a God of truth and justice when His glory was revealed in human guise in the Babe lying in a manger, and who on a cross was to marry "mercy and truth" and enable "righteousness and peace to kiss each other."

Those heavenly songsters could glorify God, for the revelation thrilled their hearts that their *Lord*, through the blood He would shed, provided sinners with justification by faith and consequently peace with God. Paul's prayer for his converts was that they might have "all joy and peace in believing" (Rom. 15:13). As for the Thessalonian church, the apostolic benediction for her members was that "the Lord of peace himself give you peace always, by all means" (2 Thess. 3:16).

Good Will toward Men

The Word becoming flesh and dwelling among men was the visible expression of the good will of God toward men. Such *good will* dates from eternity, having existed in the divine heart long before it took human form and appeared amongst men. The Incarnation, then, was "according to the eternal purpose which God purposed in Christ Jesus our Lord" (Eph. 3:11). The long-looked-for redemption came "according to the good pleasure of his will, to the praise of the glory of his grace" (Eph. 1:5, 6). God's will toward men was "good will," and fully revealed when the Son of the Highest left the heavens and, divesting

Himself of His garment of light, clothed Himself in human form. He inspired the angels thereby to rend the skies with their song of praise. The marvel is that our humanity is the robe our Redeemer wears in Heaven, and that through His grace, we have become "partakers of the divine nature"—"heirs of God, and joint-heirs with Christ" (1 Peter 1:4; Rom. 8:17).

If the fruits of Redemption: "Glory to God . . . peace on earth . . . good will among men" employed angels' songs, should they not be the subject of higher strains and loftier raptures on the part of those who, having received Jesus as their personal Savior, strive to honor Him as Christ the Lord? So, Canon Bell forcefully reminds us:

> Thus praising God we shall be in harmony with those celestial hosts, who, leaving their station before the throne of God, and speeding downwards from star to star, hovered over the stable at Bethlehem; and as they anticipated the triumphs which the Divine Babe was to win, men saved, death destroyed, the Devil vanquished, and Creation redeemed, gave vent to the joy in the jubilant song: "Glory to God in the highest, on earth peace, good will toward men."

Attention must be drawn to the paragraph found in Jamieson's *Commentary on the Whole Bible*, most worthy of repetition:

> A brief but transporting hymn—not only I articulate human speech, for our behoof, but in tunable measure, in the form of a Hebrew parallelism of two complete clauses, and a third one only amplifying the second, and so with a connecting *and*. The "Glory to God," which the new-born Saviour was to bring, is the first note of this sublime hymn; to this answers, in the second clause, the "peace on earth" of which He was to be "the Prince" (Isa. 9:6)—probably sung responsively by the celestial choir; while quick follows the glad echo of this note, probably by a third detachment of the angelic choristers—"Good will toward men." Bengel says, "They say not, glory to God in heaven, where the angels are, but, using a rare expression, *in the highest* (heavens), whither angels aspire not" (Heb. 1:3, 4).

Peace with God is the grand necessity of a lost world. To bring this in, and all other peace in its train, was the prime errand of the Saviour to this earth, and, along with it, Heaven's whole "good will to man"—the Divine complacency on a new footing—descends to rest upon men, as upon the Son Himself, in whom God is "well-pleased" (Matt. 3:17, the same word as here).[5]

We cannot meditate upon the carol sung by angels on that first Christmas day without thinking of the tragic contrast between that carol introducing the Christian faith and the fearful condition of the world today after almost 2,000 years of Christianity. What a God-rejecting age rather than a God-glorifying one we live in! Among the teeming millions of earth, few have any desire to reecho the first line of the angels' song. Lands like China and Russia with some one thousand million souls have destroyed God—so they think—through the cruel and brutal system of atheistic communism.

Throughout the rest of the world, particularly in so-called Christian nations, there is a practical assumption that if there is a God, He is far removed from our human life; that one may live without reference to Him for the needs of life; that, actually, He is not required. Such pagan secularism contends that Christianity, with its preeminent basic concept of glorifying God in the highest, is one for monks and nuns to adopt in their monastic life.

The angels who sang the message from heaven of "good will toward men," must sob as they look down on human society and see how it is now characterized by "ill will toward men." Cheerfully, the angels thought of man becoming one holy, happy family, but it must make them weep as they realize that it appears to be a sin among men, not to think alike cheerfully of themselves and others. *Good will* is a scarce commodity in human relations today. Violence, hijacking, robbery, kidnapping, deceit, jealousy, suspicion, and killings are widespread in so-called civilized countries. Even among professing Christians, good will is a virtue not practiced as it should be. Then, think of the ghastly murders in Ireland, and of the cruel, inhuman treatment of those who dare protest for liberty of conscience, and who, conse-

---

[5] Jamieson, et. al., *Commentary*, 99.

quently, are made to suffer most terrible, cruel torture in prison camps, as recent revelations in Russia and Chile have proved.

Man's inhumanity to man,
Makes countless numbers (both *angels* and men) mourn!

As for "peace on earth," what a misnomer this line in the joyful songsters' birthday hymn is in our twentieth century. The musical word—*peace*—is a promise full of victory, but since it was sung by the angelic choristers the history of the world has been written in blood. Our earth today is distracted by wars and rumors of wars, bred in the wild passions and unsanctified lusts and ambitions of men. All nations are arming themselves to the teeth because of fears of each other. *Peace!* Why, even the church seems to be "a house divided against itself," full of the din of controversy and strife; torn asunder by factious divisions and unseemly contentions over various issues, principally theological.

But, blessed be God, we are assured that swords will yet be beaten into ploughshares and spears into pruning hooks. While the vision of a peaceful world tarries, the angels' song will yet be echoed in every land, for "the earth shall be filled with the knowledge of the Lord, as the waters cover the sea" (Isa. 11:9). When the Prince of Peace appears, a restored and regenerated earth will raise the seraphic anthem to heaven, "Glory to God in the highest, on earth peace, good will toward men."

The Temptation of Jesus

It is to be regretted that the doings and sayings of these wonderful, ministering spirits have not claimed the reverent attention they should have received. The fascinating subject of angelic ministrations has fallen out of notice and that to a degree which is somewhat strange, considering how Jesus Himself was ministered unto by angels, and how frequently He referred to the "sending of angels" that His Father's purposes might be fulfilled. Did He not represent these celestial hosts as eternal, sympathizing witnesses of all that passes on in heaven and in earth? Are they not charged by God to keep the saints in all their way; and have they not a glory all their own? When Jesus, as the Son of man, comes in judgment, it will be "in his own glory, and in his Father's *and* in the holy angels'" (Luke 9:26).

In our coverage of the temptation of Jesus we touched upon the comforting, strengthening aid He received *after* the contest with the devil. All through His experience in the wilderness, however, Jesus had no recourse to His deity, or to angel for help and relief. As Jamieson and Fausset state it, "After having refused to claim the *illegitimate* ministration of angels in His behalf, with what deep joy He would accept their services when sent, unasked, at the close of all this temptation, direct from Him whom He had so gloriously honoured." But as soon as His exhausting encounter with the apostate angel was over, He gladly welcomed the beneficial ministration of the army of heaven. "Behold, angels came and ministered unto him" (Matt. 4:11). The only matter we seek to raise in this section is, what kind of angelic service was it that Jesus received, once the defeated devil had left Him?

Witnessing Him whom they had known, loved, worshipped and obeyed since His creation of them, the holy angels must have been deeply moved as they beheld Jesus as the Man, weak and hungry because of His long fast, enduring such temptation. We can rest assured, however, that those heavenly helpers mutually planned how they would assist Him in His worn-out condition once the devil had left Him. Their heartfelt and direct purpose was to bring Jesus necessary supplies for the refreshment of His weak and wearied humanity. With what exact provisions they "ministered unto him," we are not particularly informed. The original words used appear to suggest the spreading of a table for him by the angels, in the presence of His enemies. The term *ministered* is used in connection with the supply of material sustenance (Mark 1:31; Luke 8:3).

Elijah of old, when hungry, was furnished with food by an angel who evidently was able to make good nourishing cakes, enabling the prophet to continue his journey "unto the mount of God" (1 Kings 19:6–8).

Whatever the nature of "angel's food," it was a repast that relieved and refreshed the Lord of angels, and as He partook of it He doubtless heard a voice from heaven saying yet once again, "This is my beloved Son in whom I am well pleased" (Matt. 3:17; 17:5; Mark 1:11; 9:7; Luke 3:22; 9:35; 2 Peter 1:17). But do we really grasp that ours is a greater privilege in our temptations? After His conquest of the tempter, Jesus had angels to aid, dress and cook for Him, but *in* and *after* our encounters with the devil and evil forces, we have Jesus *Himself* to rally to our help and need. As we emerge victorious from a wrestle with satanic principalities and powers, heaven smiles, succors, and sustains the faithful heart, and the stress and strain of trial is more than repaired by the gracious, willing ministries of Him who is ever at hand to undertake.

Is this not the truth taught us in that great passage in Hebrews, "For in that he himself hath suffered being tempted, he is able to succour them that are tempted" (2:18). The word *succour* implies to run at the cry of help, or to advance in aid of anyone, and occurs in only one other place in the New Testament, "In the day of salvation have I succoured thee (2 Cor. 6:2). Since He was tempted "like unto his brethren" He has special ability and willingness to come to the aid of those who are tempted—because of His sympathy, His knowledge of the help needed, and by His position of High Priest which He gained through suffering. Having been tempted in *all* points as we are, He is able to succour us in an even more perfect way than angels in all possible trials and temptations common to man (Heb. 4:16; 5:2). Not only as God does He know our trials, but also as Man He knows them by experiential feeling. His holy example during temptation exhibited the way in which we, too, can be victorious, namely, by the skillful use of Scripture, suffering according to the will of God, assured that by His mighty Spirit and by the beneficial visitations and ministrations of His angels He will aid and deliver us.

> If Christ is mine, I need not fear
> The rage of earth and hell;
> He will support by feeble frame,
> Their utmost force repel.

The Agony of Jesus

While all four Gospels mention Christ's agony in the Garden, it is Luke who adds three particulars unnoticed by the other three:

1. There appeared an angel from heaven to strengthen Him.
2. That being in an agony, He prayed more earnestly.
3. That His sweat was, as it were, great drops of blood falling to the ground (Luke 22:13, 14; compare Matt. 26:36–46; Mark 14:32–42; John 18:1, 2).

As we are discovering in this section of our study, one of the mysteries of godliness which Paul mentions connected with "God manifest in flesh" was His being "seen by angels." We do not know if the multitude of angels who witnessed and welcomed His birth, or the company selected to minister to His needs *after* His temptation, were beholders of His agony in the Garden of Gethsemane. If they were, then they must have been moved with deep pity for their suffering Lord. Being capable of joy, the angels are also capable of grief, and much grief must have been theirs as they witnessed His bloody sweat accompanied by "strong crying and tears."

The Son of God in tears,
Angels with wonder see,
Be thou astonished, O my soul,
He shed those tears for thee!

The extreme anguish Jesus experienced, however, occasioned the visitation of a specially designated angel from heaven, so one was sent, probably Gabriel, who is depicted as standing in God's presence awaiting His call. He it was who announced the birth of Jesus, and who is now honored to indicate that all the heavenly host was with Jesus in the battles of heaven against sin and Hell. But before dealing with the exact way this privileged angel consoled and strengthened Jesus, I will make a brief reference to the solemn circumstances necessitating the ministration of the heavenly visitant.

In a most vehement way Jesus described that anguish of the soul which is the soul of anguish found in His heart-rending cry, "My soul is exceeding sorrowful, even unto death" (Matt. 26:38; Mark 14:34). *Even unto death*—not the pre-ordained, predicted death of the cross, but the fear that He might die before that final triumph at Calvary. Jesus was amazed, heavily oppressed, and crushed with sorrow over the events of previous days, culminating in the tragic betrayal of Judas, one of the Twelve He chose. This produced the anguish of heart that made Jesus say, in effect, "I feel as if nature would sink under the load, or as if life were ebbing out and death coming before its time."

Timpson reminds us of what many commentators of a past century suggested: in this extreme suffering of our Lord, He struggled with legions of the spirits of darkness; that He was surrounded with a mighty host of devils, who exercised all their force and malice to persecute and distract His innocent soul. They imagine that Satan hoped, or at least endeavored, by overpowering Him with his agents in Gethsemane, to have prevented the fulfillment of the divine prophecies relating to the manner of the redeemer's death, and so to have defeated the design of our redemption.

Elsewhere, we have drawn attention to the efforts of the devil, who had the power of death, to kill Jesus before He reached the cross to die by crucifixion (as both psalmist and prophet portrayed long before such a cruel mode of death for criminals was invented by the Romans). Do the terms, "exceeding sorrowful unto death"—"being in an agony"—"sweating, as it were, great drops of blood," indicate that the Garden was the devil's last attempt to end the life of Jesus before the surrender of such a life to the death of the cross? Was this part of the mixture of the cup He prayed might pass from Him, seeing He had declared that no man—or devil for that matter—was able to take His life from Him? As redemption could only be purchased at the costly price Paul calls "the blood of God" (Acts 20:28), then, the death He was born to die was one none could nullify.

It is somewhat significant that as Jesus reached Gethsemane, He said to His disciples, "Pray (Matthew adds *watch*) that ye enter not into temptation"—a temptation He Himself was about to face (Luke 22:40, 46). Temptation presupposes figures and forces that tempt. Matthew Henry comments that "in the Garden Christ entered the lists with the powers of darkness, and yet conquered them." The plea of Jesus, however, is a reecho of the prayer He taught his disciples to pray: "Lead us not into temptation, but deliver us from evil." He was referring to the evil lurking in the temptation. The disciples now see the clause used in all the fullness of its meaning, as Jesus enters a season of trial and suffering from which He would not shrink. As a man, Jesus felt the need of company to console Him in His hour of conflict, and so requested of His followers, "Tarry ye here, and watch with me" (Matt. 26:38; Mark 14:34). But they failed Him, preferring sleep to a vigilant watch. They slept as He suffered. Not so the alert angel who came to His aid not *after* His season of spiritual, bodily, and mental exertion, but *during* it. Gabriel, along with his God and our God, and all the angels, "neither slumber nor sleep" (Ps. 121:4).

The wonder is that as Jesus bore "a weight of woe more than ten worlds could bear," He did not draw upon His reserve of deity to strengthen and sustain Him in that grim experience, but accepted the assistance of an angel. Being made "lower than the angels" in His humiliation, He was capable of receiving help from one of them. Thus, as the surges rose higher, beating more tempestuously until it seemed as if they would overcome Him, in the bitterness of His feared death, the angel appeared to fortify Him, to brace up His sinking form in His anticipation and rehearsal of the final struggle. Victory must be His "now on the theatre of *an invincible will*; then on the arena of the Cross. *I will suffer* is the grand result of Gethsemane: *It is finished* is the shout that bursts from the Cross."

While the disciples proved themselves to be "miserable comforters" (Job 16:2), broken reeds, the solicitous seraph was "strengthening him," Luke tells us (22:43). Although several commentators have made conjectures as to the form or nature of the strength imparted, Luke does not give us any particulars as to the angelic messenger's ministry of love to the suffering Redeemer. What is clear is the varied meaning in the original of the word "strengthen." Shortly before entering the Garden Jesus urged His disciples to *strengthen* one another, and here the word means "to fix firmly," "to make steadfast" (Luke 22:32). But the word for the *strength* the angel ministered is different, and implies to "in-strengthen, invigorate, make strong." For the assistance of Jesus against the powers of darkness, the angel from heaven, evidently in a visible form, stood by Him and invigorated Him by the sensible token of the Father's protection and favor, and by suggesting holy consolations calculated to animate His soul in such a struggle.

A comment from the last century as to the angel's aid suggests, "Perhaps he wiped away His sweat and tears, ministered some cordial to Him, as after the Temptation or, it may be, took Him by the arm, and helped Him off the ground, or bore Him up when He was ready to faint away; and in this service of the angel, the Holy Spirit was *putting strength into Him*; for so the word signifies." Whatever the comforts were the angel ministered to relieve Jesus in His human anguish, He was pleased to receive such from one of His creation, just as God receives glory from His creatures. That the angelic aid was beneficial is seen in the way Jesus responded, after He had been raised up from the cold ground, had His fainting head supported, and the bloody sweat washed from His deathlike face.

"Rise; let us be going!" (Matt. 26:16). Jesus appeared fresh and glorious in His visage. *Rise!* as if filled with renewed courage after having defeated a savage foe. Such was the effect of the angel's ministry, that those who came to apprehend Jesus as He emerged from the Garden, fell backward to the ground, as He presented Himself and simply said, "I am he" (John 18:5). The lesson we learn from the interposition of the angel as he saw and strengthened Jesus, is that when human comforters fail, as His disciples left Him alone; when our nearest friends fail in ability to render us needful aid, heavenly ministering forces are at hand to succor and comfort—that God Himself as "the God of all comfort" will be the strength of our hearts and our portion for ever.

The Resurrection of Jesus

Scripture is silent as to whether, when Jesus was dying (in the eyes of a godless world, as a felon on a wooden gibbet) He was seen by angels. We have no record of an angel appearing for His rescue or relief when, as the Man of Sorrows, He carried the load of the world's guilt, and by being "stricken, smitten of God, and afflicted" (Isa. 53:4), made reconciliation for iniquity. Yet because there is joy in the presence of the celestial spirits over one sinner repenting, there must have been praise among them as they received the news of Christ's first fruit of His death as the sinless Substitute for sinners, in the salvation of His fellow sufferer, the dying thief, who rejoiced to see the fountain for sin and uncleanness opened in his day. But once Jesus, who could not be holden of death, arose, the angles were at the tomb, not only to guard His lifeless body while it reposed therein, but to announce His resurrection to life, even as they had celebrated His entrance into our life at birth.

As a dramatic introduction to the most outstanding miracle of history, God caused a supernatural earthquake in Jerusalem, which shook the entire city and caused the inhabitants to reflect upon their crime in having "crucified the Lord of Glory," and likewise prepared the way for the angelic announcement of His victorious triumph over the grave and Satan. Such a convulsion must have also struck terror into the hearts of the Roman guards, as the rocking earth made them "stagger like a drunken man" (Job 12:25; Ps. 107:27). In their consternation they sought to ascertain the mysterious cause of the earth tremor, and they were immediately arrested by the visible presence of a heavenly being who had been sent by the omnipotent God, as His official from the Court of His Palace.

Those imperial guards, and all the formidable weapons of the Roman army, were no match for an angel armed with the might of God. Vainly did the soldiers defend the sacred tomb of Jesus, for that one angel was well able to roll away the great stone sealing its entrance preventing, thereby, any attempt to steal the nail-scarred body (Matt. 27:65–66). Military array and destructive weapons employed to defend the burial place were useless against the angel of the Lord who rolled back the stone, beyond the strength of a human to remove, *and sat upon it.* What ignominy that must have been to proud Rome to see an angel making a seat of the stone, sitting at ease, in defiance of the mightiest legions of the then mistress of the world. Seated with perfect composure, as a servant in waiting, the angel, in effect, was saying to the armed guards: "You may retire from your present charge, and report what has now transpired: for I design to remain here on guard, to wait upon Jesus, who was crucified, and to fulfill the orders of my injured Master."

This fearless guardian angel is described by Mark as "a young man" (16:5), with a "countenance like lightning, and his raiment white as snow; and for fear of him the keepers did shake, and became as dead men" (Matt. 28:3, 4). "Lightning dressed like snow," is reckoned to be the finest expression which human language can furnish to describe the appearance of an inhabitant of heaven. How dull, then, must the splendor of this world appear, and how mean its finest dresses before the brilliant lustre of an angel clothed in his spotless robe! How glorious and terrible to guilty mortals must the appearance of angels be. Good men like Daniel, Manoah, and other holy persons have been overwhelmed by the splendor and unable to bear the sight of them without trembling.

The two words that stand out in the description of this dazzling angel are *countenance* and *raiment*, the former expressing the *glory*, the latter, the *purity* of the glorious and holy abode from which he came. The prostrate condition of those dreaded Roman warriors indicates what effect the brilliant angel had on them. In the words of the psalmist, "The stout-hearted are spoiled, they have slept their sleep: and none of the men of might have found their hands" (Ps. 76:5). To identify the angels who witnessed the Resurrection: we have the angel just mentioned who not only rolled away the stone of the tomb but announced the Resurrection to the women who had arrived early at the place of burial (Matt. 28:5–7); the two angels who guarded the tomb and introduced the risen Lord to Mary Magdalene (John 20:11–14); the testimony of what took place at the Resurrection was rendered by a vision of angels (Luke 24:23).

Mary, who feared that some strange thing may have happened to the body of her precious Lord, wept at the sepulchre, and stooping down, looked into it, and through her tears saw two angels in white sitting, "the one at the head, and the other at the feet, where the body of Jesus had lain" (John 20:12). These angelic guardians had been watching that body that had housed "God manifest in flesh." Emphasis is on the words, *had lain*, but He was not there, as Mary came to learn when she met her risen Master alive forevermore. Is it not moving to observe that the first words of Jesus after His glorious victory were directed to "devote a love that had all along been shown toward Him, and when Mary fully recognized Him, cried excitedly *Rabboni*! She had heard in the well-known voice her own name, and it brought back to her all the old associations."

What stupendous news the dazzling, angelic herald flashed to heaven and earth, and even to *hell*!

"He is not here: for he is risen, as he said" (Matt. 28:6).
He is not here—The Empty Tomb
He is risen—The Eternal Triumph
As He said—The Established Truth

He Is Not Here!

It is most beneficial for us that He was not there, for had the grave continued to possess His dead body, we would have been of all men most miserable, having no salvation, no hope of eternal life. Paul tells us that if Jesus had remained in the tomb, then *preaching* and *faith* would be vain (1 Cor. 15:12–20). What a charming invitation the angel gave to the women who had come to pay their respect to the dead, "Come, see the place where the Lord lay" (Matt. 28:6). But He was no longer in the place where they had seen a friend lay Him, and how amazed they must have been to hear the assuring angel say, "Come, see the place where the Lord of glory lay: now it is an empty grave: He lies not here, but He *lay* there. Come, feast your eyes upon it!"

Had death kept its prey another day, the corruption which ordinarily ensues in a dead body would have set in. Martha, sister of dead Lazarus, said to Jesus when He visited the grave at Bethany, "Lord, by this time he stinketh, for he hath been dead four days"—the offensive smell being proof that decomposition had set in (John 11:39). But the prophecy regarding Jesus was that God would not suffer the body of His Holy One to remain in the grave nor see corruption, so He was raised from the dead on the third day, and thus saw no corruption (Ps. 16:10, 11; Acts 2:31; 13:35–37).

It is impossible to fix the exact moment when Jesus burst the bars of death, and rose triumphant, but the indications are that it was about sunrise. The Marys came to the sepulchre "as it began to dawn" (Matt. 28:1, 5). Ellicott remarks that "there was an obvious fitness in the symbolism of the Resurrection of the Son of Righteousness coinciding with the natural *Day-Spring* (Luke 1:78)."[6]

He Has Risen!

The empty tomb, and the angel's positive declaration, testify to the most glorious fact of our Christian faith. On the Lord's Day, and on every day, we should praise the Lord for His eternal victory over sin, death, and the devil; and we should rejoice in such a birthday of all our hopes. As that eminent divine and poet, Doddridge, expressed it:

---

[6]Ellicott, *Commentary.*

Now is the justice of God amply satisfied, or the prisoner had never been released. Now is the reproach of the Cross ceased, and turned into proportionable glory. That reproach was rolled away at once by the descending angel, who appeared, not to awaken Christ from His sleep, but bring Him a new life; but to add a solemn pomp to His revival, and to strike the guards with such a terror as would prevent any mad attempt on this glorious Conqueror, when bursting the bonds of death. "Now is Christ *indeed* risen from the dead, and become the firstfruits of them that slept" (1 Cor. 15:20).

No wonder Paul concludes his marvelous exposition on the resurrection of Christ with the glorious crescendo:

Death is swallowed up in victory.
O death, where is thy sting?
O grave, where is thy victory? (1 Cor. 15:54, 55).

In poetic form Doddridge summarizes the witness and ministry of the angels in connection with the Resurrection in the lines:

Lo! the angelic bands
In full assembly meet,
To wait His high commands,
And worship at His feet:
Joyful they come, and wing their way,
From realms of day to such a tomb!
Then back to Heaven they fly,
And the glad tidings bear:
Hark! as they soar on high,
What music fills the air!
Their anthems say, "Jesus has bled,
Hath left the dead: He rose to-day . . . "

As He Said!

Rising again from the dead, Jesus verified or established the veracity of ancient predictions, as well as His own, to His everlasting conquest of death. As He said! What had He said regarding His ignominious death and glorious Resurrection? Listen to His masterly challenge: "I have power to lay it down, and I have power to take it again" (John 10:18). "I have power to lay it down (His life)." At Calvary, this is what He did, for His death was voluntary. His life was not *taken* but *given*. He died not as victim but as Victor.

"I have power to take it again," meaning that He rose again by His own volition as the Son of God with power. He also said that the Holy Spirit was the Source of His power during His ministry as a Man among men. Rome had placed the imperial seal on the heavy stone closing the tomb, and also in the might of her warriors who were there to see that Jesus did not rise again, but God had His Seal inside assuring that His Son would rise again. Is not the Holy Spirit the Divine Seal? So God raised up Jesus from the dead (Rom. 6:14; Acts 2:24). Luke tells us that the women who came early to the sepulchre testified that they had seen a vision of angels who announced that Jesus was alive (Luke 24:10).

The important aspect of our meditation is expressed by Paul in the words, "Like as Christ was raised from the dead by the glory of the Father, even so we also may walk in newness of life" (Rom. 6:4). If we thus share His risen life then "He that raised up Christ from the dead shall also quicken your mortal bodies by his Spirit who dwelleth in us" (Rom. 8:11; see also Phil. 3:10, 11; Col. 3:1). The pertinent, angelic question asked of the women as they came with their spices to anoint the slain body of the Lord has a practical application for all who claim to be risen with Christ. "Why seek ye the living among the dead?" (Luke 24:5). The margin has it, "Why seek him that liveth among the dead?"

In the days of his flesh, Jesus uttered a like parallel in the command, "Let the dead bury their dead" (Matt. 8:22). For the sorrowing women who came to the tomb such a question was enough to change the whole current of their thoughts. The Lord whom they came to honor as dead was in very deed "living." He was emphatically "He that liveth," and as Jesus Himself says from the glory, "alive for evermore" (Rev. 1:18). He that was dead, but now "ever liveth," does not expect to find those who are "partakers of his resurrection" among the dead things of the world, or in dead works. If we are risen with Him, then we must seek those things above, and not be found among worldly ambitions and amusements of a world dead in sin. Worldly-minded

Christians need to be reminded of what it truly means to be risen with Him who left the place of the dead behind Him.

The Ascension of Jesus

Witnessing the glorious Ascent of Jesus was the climax of the beatific vision of the angels. The solemn parting from His disciples on earth was seen by angels. Peter reminds us that "the glory that should follow" the sufferings of Christ, was a messianic theme the angels desired to look into (1 Peter 1:12). How their minds, then, would be fully satisfied with the revelation of this mystery of godliness as they not only gazed upon their ascending Lord, but also accompanied Him on His return to the glory which he had had with the Father "before the world began" (2 Tim. 1:9; Titus 1:2). The Ascension was a wonderful confirmation of the Incarnation.

While Luke definitely states that there were two angels in assumed human form covered with white apparel attending our Lord's ascent, the question remains whether there were other angelic companions on that triumphal return to the Father's home (Acts 1:10–11). As He rose from earth, by His own divine power, in a manner worthy of His majesty, as the "Lord of Glory" who had been "God manifest in flesh," we are told that "a cloud received him out of their sight" (Acts 1:9), causing the awestruck disciples to lose sight of their beloved Master. Such a brilliant cloud not only signified the splendour of His glorious body, but may also represent a heaven-sent guard of angels, seeing that the appearance of angels is sometimes described by a cloud. The Lord of Angels said that He would appear in the cloud upon the mercy seat, where sat the two cherubim (Lev. 16:2). Daniel has the prophecy that One "like the Son of man came with clouds of heaven . . . and they brought him near before him" (7:13).

While recent translators remove the most expressive phrase from the A.V. narrative of the ascension account, "carried up into heaven," one loves to feel that this actually happened, and a host of angels bore Him up as in a conqueror's chair, to realms above, there to be welcomed by ten thousand times ten thousand more angelic voices singing in adoration and worship, "Worthy is I the Lamb that was slain to receive power . . . honour, and glory, and blessing" (Rev. 5:12). David wrote of "The chariots of God are twenty thousand, even thousands of angels" (Ps. 68:17). Gregg has the lines:

> They brought His chariot from above,
> To bear Him to His throne;
> Spread their triumphant wings, and sang
> "The glorious work is done!"

When it came to Elijah's dramatic ascension, he did not rise in as elegant, majestic fashion as Jesus, but was snatched away in a whirlwind, *in a chariot of fire*, with fiery horses—a departure suited to that stern reprover of an apostate race.

Further, those angels knew that the glory given to Christ at His ascension—a glory which flowed from the cross—was conferred on Him, not in His divine nature, for as God He could not be further exalted, but because of His mediatorial work as "the man Christ Jesus." The angelic investigation of the sufferings of Christ, Peter mentions, included the love of God, as revealed at Calvary, for a lost world. The angels knew that "God is love," as their own creation and happiness proved, but for Him to love sinful man, and to surrender His Son for the propitiation of man's sins, caused them to marvel. The immeasurable love of Christ surpassed all knowledge—a love manifested nowhere else in such unspeakable greatness and sacrifice was certainly one aspect of the divine nature they worthily desired "to look into." Jesus had been made a little lower than the angels for the suffering of death but He was now crowned with glory and honor and given a name above any other name, and in joy unspeakable and full of glory (Eph. 6:21; Heb. 12:2).

Although Jesus was leaving His disciples—His church's representation, and embryo, on earth—He was not to be detached from them. While the angels joyfully and adoringly welcomed His public entry into the *Jerusalem above*, He Himself revealed that He had at heart the concerns of His church to be established, and so sent two angels in white apparel to assure His disciples that although He had been taken out of their midst, they would see Him return in like manner as He went to heaven (Acts 1:11). While with them He had promised that they would share His heavenly abode, "I will come again, and receive you unto myself; that *where I am*, there ye may be also" (John 14:3). How, then, must the faith of the men of Galilee have been confirmed, and their hearts comforted, to hear the twin angels announce, "*This same Jesus . . .* shall so come in like manner as ye have seen him go into heaven" (Acts 1:11). He who had just left them would be the very same One to return, a prophetic revelation Paul elaborated on when he wrote that "*The Lord himself* shall descend from heaven" (1 Thess. 4:16). Then the apostle went on to record that at the Rapture of the true church, angels will again be the attendants for the descending Lord, for their musical shout will be heard, and the silvery voice of the archangel, possibly Gabriel who proclaimed Christ's First Advent, will publish His Second Advent (Acts 1:10, 11; 1 Thess. 4:13–18). So, when the redeemed meet the Lord in the air on their ascension to glory, they, too will be *seen of angels*. We know of no other way to conclude our meditation of this fourth line of the triumphant hymn of the early church, than that of the repetition in full of Gregg's impressive poem, written over a hundred years ago:

> Beyond the glittering starry skies,
> Far as the eternal hills,
> Yon heaven of heavens with living light,
> Our great Redeemer fills.
>
> Legions of angels, strong and fair,
> In countless armies shine;
> And swell his praises with golden harps,
> Attuned to songs divine.
>
> "Hail Prince!" they cry, "for ever hail!"
> Whose unexampled love—
> Moved thee to quit those glorious realms
> And royalties above.
>
> Through all his travels here below,
> They did his steps attend;
> Oft wondering how and where at last,
> The mystic scene would end.

They saw his heart transfix'd with wounds,
With love and grief run o'er:
They saw him break the bars of death,
Which none e'er brake before.

They brought his chariot from above,
To bear him to His throne;
Spread their triumphant wings, and sang,
"The glorious work is done!"

The Teachings of Jesus

If the angels had a great deal to do with Jesus in the days of his flesh, He certainly had much to say about their nature and ministry in His public teaching. Much as we would like to linger over an exposition of this aspect of study, the same is not within the province of coverage of the creedal chant we are considering. But for the guidance of those who desire to pursue such a profitable theme, we herewith append James Hastings' outline to follow on these intermediaries between God and man:

1. Their dwelling place is in heaven (Matt. 18:46; Luke 42:8, 9; John 1:51).

2. They are superior to men, but in the world to come the righteous shall be on equality with them (Luke 20:34).

3. They carry away the souls of the righteous to a place of rest (Luke 16:22).

4. They are (as seems to be suggested) of neither sex (Matt. 22:30).

5. They are very numerous (Matt. 26:53).

6. They will appear with Christ at His Second Advent. Most of His references to angels are associated with this truth (Matt. 13:39; 16:27; 24:31; 25:31; Mark 8:38; Luke 9:26).

7. There are bad as well as good angels (Matt. 25:41). It is usually of the latter that reference is made.

8. They are limited in knowledge (Matt. 24:36).

9. There are guardian angels of children (Matt. 18:10).

10. They rejoice at the triumph of good (Luke 15:10).

5

HIS PROCLAMATION

Preached unto the Gentiles (1 Tim. 3:16)

The above suggested translation of this portion of the very early Christian hymn we are considering, coupled with the past tense "preached," definitely links the proclamation with the second line, "God was manifest in the flesh," and covers the ministry of Christ and His apostles. It would take volumes to record the great multitudes of Gentiles saved by Grace through the preaching of the glorious gospel (which the incarnation of Christ made possible) since the Apostolic Age. If Paul wrote First Timothy around A.D. 65, this means that he was covering some thirty-five years from the entrance of Jesus into His public ministry up to the time Paul penned his Epistle.

It is generally known that, in Scripture, *Gentiles*, *nations*, *heathen*, *peoples*, *Greeks*, and *strangers*, are equivalent terms. When Paul reminded the Ephesians that in time past, as Gentiles, they were "strangers from the covenant of promise" as well as "aliens," (Eph. 2:12) he fully and fittingly described their distinction from Jews. If the A.V. word *Gentiles* is retained, the antithesis will be between the *angels* who are so *near* to the Son of God, the Lord of angels, and the *Gentiles* who were so utterly "afar off" from Him (Eph. 2:17).

In the Old Testament, the Gentiles were those who were not of Israel. In the New Testament, they were those who were neither of Israel nor of the church (1 Cor. 10:32). In Christ there is neither Jew nor Gentile. In this age of grace, the true church is composed of both Jews and Gentiles, born anew by the Holy Spirit. They are no longer known as distinct nationalities, but as one in Christ Jesus. God does not look down upon men and segregate them nationally. To Him they are all alike sinners needing to be saved in the same way by the same Savior. "*All* have sinned, and come short of the glory of God" (Rom. 3:23).

That the Gentiles figure largely in the New Testament is proven by the fact that the term itself occurs some 100 times and that whether cannibal or civilized, they can be delivered from their sin and made part of the mystic fabric, the church of the Living God. Thus, Dummelow in his *Bible Commentary* paraphrases the Pauline statement of Ephesians 2:11–22:

> The Gentiles were formerly cut off from Israel and from God's promises. But now Christ's death has broken down the barrier between Gentile and Jew, and reconciled both as one body to God. There are now no strangers: all are fellow-citizens; all are part of a spiritual temple, in which God in His Spirit dwells.[1]

The history of gentile dominion (from its commencement around 600 B.C. when Nebuchadnezzar, the then King of the mighty Babylonian Empire, subdued Jerusalem through the force of arms, right on till its consummation when Christ returns as King of Kings, and Lord or Lords, to make the kingdoms of this world His own world-kingdom) is a subject of absorbing interest. Since it is, however, beyond the scope of the phrase we are presently considering, we must reluctantly desist from pursuing it. Suffice it to say, however, that the might of the Gentiles was *carnal*, while that of Israel was *spiritual*. Gentile monarchy puts its trust in princes, horses, and chariots; but Israel's trust was in the Lord. For the Gentile, it was the arm of flesh—for Israel, the arm of the Lord. Rudyard Kipling, in his marvelous *Recessional*, has this stirring stanza:

> If, drunk with sight of power, we loose
> Wild tongues that have not Thee in awe,
> Such boastings as the Gentiles use,
> Or lesser breeds without the Law,

---

[1] Dummelow, *Commentary*, 962.

For heathen heart that puts her trust
In reeking tube and iron shard,
All valiant dust that builds on dust,
And, guarding, calls not Thee to guard,
For frantic boast and foolish word—
Thy mercy on Thy People, Lord!

The differing ideologies between Gentiles and Jews (and that which kept them apart) has been well summarized for us in *The Bible Encyclopedia and Dictionary*:

> With all the superiority of the Gentile great world kingdoms, in military prowess, commerce, luxury, and the fine arts, Israel stood on an immense moral elevation above them, in the one point *nearness* to *God*, and possession of His revealed will and Word, Exod. 19:5, 6; Ps. 147:19, 20; 148:14; Rom. 3:1, 2. But this superiority was in order that Israel, as priests unto God, might be mediator of blessings unto all nations (Isa. 61:6). The covenant from the first with Abraham contemplated that "in his seed all the nations of the earth should be blessed." Genesis 22:18.

It was because of this religious distinction that the Jews were forbidden to fellowship with Gentiles. Children born of mixed marriages between Jews and Gentiles were reckoned as *bastards*. This is what caused the Jews to be so hated by Greeks and Romans as the writings of Cicero and Seneca reveal (see John 18:28; Acts 10:28; 11:3). While the Old Testament predicts salvation for *all* nations, the emphasis is upon the salvation of Israel through the coming of her Messiah, and of her inclusion in God's redemption scheme. Thus, many like "just and devout" Simeon waited for "the consolation of Israel," and with godly Anna "looked for redemption in Jerusalem" (Luke 2:25, 38).

The New Testament opens with the declaration that Jesus was born "to save *his people* from their sins" (Matt. 1:21); that He was the horn of salvation raised up from the house of David for His people whom He had come to redeem (Luke 1:68–71). Jesus came as "the glory of thy people Israel" (Luke 2:32). But although Jesus came unto His own people, the Jews, they received Him not. Often He would have gathered them under His wings for protection, but as He Himself wailed, "*Ye would not!*" (Matt. 23:37). The Gospels are a long record of the hatred of the Jewish hierarchy toward Him, a hatred only satisfied when they had engineered the cruel, gentile form of death for Him who was "the King of the Jews" (John 19:21).

The Jews themselves, in national pride, failed to see that through them the gentile nations were to be blessed, and in rejecting their Messiah, they were "broken off" from the olive tree, that the Gentiles might be "grafted in" (Rom. 11:11–35). Not until "the times of the Gentiles are fulfilled" (Luke 21:24) will the times of Israel begin, with a glory eclipsing her past, but lost, glory. All Israel shall be saved and the receiving of her is as "receiving . . . life from the dead (Rom. 11:2–15).

But what about the Gentiles? Such a question brings us back to the phrase, "Preached among the Gentiles." Who preached, we ask, and what message was preached? Gentiles were among the common people who heard Jesus preach, and in the throngs that pressed upon Him as He proclaimed all He had come to accomplish as the Incarnate Word. Greeks, or Gentiles, approached Phillip with the request: "Sir, we would see Jesus." Jesus told them that the hour had come for Him as God manifested in flesh, to fall into the ground and die, that He might bring forth much fruit (John 12:20–25).

There were times when Jesus appeared to share the Jewish conception of gentile exclusion from the covenant of promise. Did He not say that "Salvation is of the Jews" (John 4:22) and that He was sent to redeem "the lost sheep of the house of Israel" (Matt. 10:6)? Then there is the incident of the Syrophoenician woman whom Mark calls a *Gentile* (7:26 M.L.B.). This woman, hearing of the fame of Jesus as a preacher and healer, came to Him, brokenhearted over her demon-possessed daughter. She was met with an apparently harsh refusal for the exorcism of the evil spirit. Jesus said unto her, "Let the children (the Jews) first be filled: for it is not meet to take the children's bread, and to cast it unto the dogs (The Gentiles)" (Mark 7:27). The Jews regarded the Gentiles as *dogs*, but by unbelief they ceased to be the true Israel and themselves became *dogs* (Isa. 56:10, 11).

But this desperate plea of the distressed Gentile woman elicited great praise from Jesus, for she said to Him, "Yes, Lord; yet the dogs under the table eat of the children's crumbs" (Mark 7:28). Impressed by her reply, persistence, and faith, Jesus commended her as a woman of great faith and lifted the burden from her heart by assuring her that on her return she would find her daughter whole again. Surely, this mother will ever remain a remarkable case of faith outside Israel, and of Jesus' exceptional healing beyond the precincts of the elect nation which He had deemed to be His special sphere. Other Gentiles also heard Him preach and participated in His miraculous power, for He had come as "A light to lighten the Gentiles" as well as "the glory of thy people Israel" (Luke 2:32). He went about "healing *all* that were oppressed of the devil" (Acts 10:38).

Announcing the birth of Jesus, the angel of the Lord said that His appearance as a Babe was "good tidings of great joy, which shall be to *all* people" (Luke 2:10). Then, as He came to preach, He declared that God loved the world, made up of Jews and Gentiles, and that *whosoever* believed in Him would not perish. As Jesus was dying by a gentile method of torture, His first convert was the gentile thief, doubtless a Roman dying for crimes committed against his country. As Jesus was about to be received up into glory He commissioned His disciples to go out and teach *all* nations, all that He had accomplished by life, lip and libation (Matt. 28:19).

The Book of Acts is the dramatic evidence that the apostles obeyed and "preached through Jesus the Resurrection" (Acts 4:2) to Gentiles, as well as Jews, with astonishing results. While Pentecost, with its dynamic ministry of the Spirit, was confined to the apostles and to devout Jews, "out of every nation under heaven" (Acts 2:5), Peter could say that the promise of the Spirit was also "to all that are afar off, even as many as the Lord our God shall call" (Acts 2:39). In his preaching Peter, stressed the incarnation of his Lord, in his description of Him as "Jesus of Nazareth, a *man* approved of God," who died, rose again, and was exalted on high (Acts 2:22, 30–36; 10:34–48).

Like his Master, Peter (along with John) felt the lash of the whip, when the early Christians came to face the hostile Jewish rulers over the apostolic preaching of Jesus and His Resurrection resulting in more than 5,000 men being converted (a number probably made up of both Jews and Gentiles). Did Peter not preach, "There is none other name under heaven given among men (irrespective of race or religion) whereby we must be saved" (Acts 4:12)? Stephen was the first martyr

of the early church for preaching the words and works of Jesus of
Nazareth (Acts 6:14; 7:58).

Paul is outstanding as an apostle who preached the unsearchable
riches of Christ to Gentiles. Arrested by the Lord on his way to capture
Christian Jews and bring them bound to Jerusalem, he was to receive the
message that he was a chosen vessel unto Him who had said, "I am
Jesus whom thou persecutest," and that he was to bear His name before
the Gentiles and gentile kings, as well as to the children of Israel
(Acts 9:15). As Paul, transformed by grace, commenced his commission,
the Jews took counsel to kill him, the first of his many sufferings for His
name's sake (Acts 9:16, 23). Like his Master, Paul found himself rejected by Jewish rulers, and thus there came about his marvelous
apostleship to the Gentiles. "Lo, we turn to the Gentiles," and Paul's
preaching to the Gentiles produced remarkable results (Acts 13:44–49).
Peter, too, threw off the cloak of Jewish exclusion and became a mighty
preacher to the Gentiles (Acts 10:9–48), and with Paul preached that
"Gentiles should be fellow-heirs, and of the same body, and partakers
of his promise in Christ by the gospel," and that as "Gentiles" they
could share in "the unsearchable riches of Christ" (Eph. 3:6–8).

The early confession of faith was peculiarly the outcome of the
Pauline churches, in which Gentiles predominated. One of the glories
of the Redeemer was the way in which the preaching of His saving
gospel greatly influenced those who hitherto had sat in darkness as in
the shadow of death. "Preached among the Gentiles" was a wonderful
fulfillment of Isaiah's thrice-rejected prophecy of the Messiah's advent
as a "light to lighten the Gentiles" (42:6; 49:6; 60:3). Thus, as Ellicott
summarizes this widespread evangelization among those who were
once "aliens from the commonwealth of Israel":

> The angels now for the first time saw, and gazed on, and rejoiced
> in the vision of the Godhead manifested in the glorified humanity
> of the Son; and what the angels gained in the beatific vision, the
> nations of the world obtained through the preaching of the Gos-
> pel, namely, the knowledge of the endless love and the surpassing
> glory of Christ.[2]

---

[2]Ellicott, *Commentary.*

Since apostolic times a vast multitude of Gentiles no man can number have responded to the preaching of the Gospel of "The God incarnate born" and become new creatures in Christ Jesus—and, blessed be His name, I am one of them, for as I write these lines in 1976, it is well over seventy years since, as a lost Gentile, I heard Christ preached as the One who died for my salvation, and in the evangelistic meeting opened the avenues of my being to Him who translated me from my darkness into His marvelous light.

It is to be questioned whether the present-day church shares the passion of the early church to preach Christ, in all His fullness, to Gentiles. Out of a world population of over 3 billion, there are only some 15 million Jews, and thus millions in the Gentile world are waiting to hear of Him who came as the Light of the World. He is also the *Light* of Israel, but rejected as such. Before He can become her *Glory* in His millennial reign, her eyes must be opened to see Him whom they pierced and mourn or repent for their long, persistent rejection of Him. Evangelistic efforts must include reaching the lost in the house of Israel, and there are a score of Jewish missions active in winning Jews for Christ. But the preponderance of Gentiles all over the earth presents a challenge the church cannot escape. She must hear the bitter cry of earth's millions, "Come and help us, for we die." With urgency the Church must echo the cry:

Ye Gentile sinners, ne'er forget
The wormwood and the gall;
Go spread your trophies at His feet,
And crown Him Lord of all.[3]

---

[3] Edward Perronet, "All Hail the Power of Jesus' Name" from *New Songs for Service* (The Rodeheaver Co., 1929) 37.

6

HIS SALVATION

Believed on in the world (1 Tim. 3:16)

This sixth line the apostle quotes from a hymn of faith chanted by the church of his day is not a repetition of the previous line, "*Preached unto the Gentiles*," but correlative, with the *believing* following the *preaching* of the cross which, to all who believe, becomes the power of God unto salvation. In his Roman Epistle, Paul, declaring that there is no difference between Jew and Gentile when it comes to the gospel invitation, rings the changes on *preaching* and *believing*.

How then shall they call on him in whom they have not believed? And how shall they believe in him of whom they have not heard? And how shall they hear without a preacher? And how shall they preach, except they be sent? As it is written, "How beautiful are the feet of them that preach the gospel of peace, and bring glad tidings of good things.". . . . So then faith cometh by hearing, and hearing by the word of God (Rom. 10:14–17).

Who or *what* was believed in throughout the world up to the time Paul wrote his First Epistle to Timothy? Such a question takes us back to the second line announcing that Jesus came as God manifested in flesh; that as the Son of God He became the Son of Man for the supreme purpose of seeking and saving the lost in the world. Thus, at the heart of His Incarnation was the provision of redemption for a whole world lost in the darkness of sin. From the time of Adam's transgression, the world has lain in wickedness, and is more than ever buried in it (1 John 5:19).

In this connection it is interesting to compare Paul's 3:16 in 1 Timothy, and John's 3:16 in his Gospel. "God so loved the world, that he gave his only begotten Son, that whosoever believeth in him should not perish, but have everlasting life." From the time Jesus gave the world this most wonderful verse in Scripture, myriads have "believed on [Him] in the world"—and found in Him a personal Savior from the guilt and penalty of their sin. They proved that—

> Faith alone is the master key
> To the strait and narrow road;
> The other but skeleton pick-locks be.
> And you never shall pick the locks of God.

While here, in the days of His flesh, Jesus predicted the magnetism of His cross when He said, "I, if I be lifted up, will draw all men unto me" (John 12:32–33).

> Drawn to the Cross which Thou hast blest,
> With healing gifts for souls distrest,
> To find in Thee my Life, my Best
> Christ crucified, I come.

The religious leaders would not come unto Him that they might have life. They found Jesus a controversial figure and rejected His claims to deity, and they finally plotted His death. But while they deliberately shut their eyes to faith, the common people heard Him gladly and believed on Him. The Pharisees themselves had to confess, "Perceive ye how ye prevail nothing? behold the world is gone after him" (John 12:19). The resurrection of Lazarus from the dead brought even Gentiles from afar to see and hear Him.

When John the Baptist was put in prison, Jesus went into Galilee preaching the gospel, calling upon all and sundry to repent and believe the gospel, and before His ascension, He commissioned His disciples to go out into all the world and preach the gospel as He had to every creature—which they did with the following signs of many believing in the crucified, risen, and exalted Savior when they preached.

In passing, a word is necessary concerning two statements John makes, namely, "God so loved the world" (John 3:16), and "Love not the world" (1 John 2:15). There is, of course, no contradiction between these two phrases, for the true believer loves what God loves. When the apostle of love tells us not to love the world, he refers to *things* in the world, as he goes on to state. These things in the world are its pleasures, pastimes, pursuits, and policies. The world, as a sphere, to live in, is a corrupt place, but grace can be ours to live as those who are not of this world. Those who live thus are those who do believe that the Father sent His Son into the world to die for their salvation (John 17:23, 25).

For those redeemed by the blood, the world is a shadow, an enemy's domain, seeing that the devil is the god it follows; it is the world that crucified Jesus, and it is detrimental to life and character to be too intimate with its worldly inhabitants. The world of *things* is to be treated as vapor, appearing for a little, then vanishing away, and the saint's determination should be, "There is none upon earth I desire beside thee."

> Lord, from this world call off my love,
> Set my affections right,
> Bid me aspire to joys above,
> And walk no more by sight.

But in the greatest text in the Bible, when John wrote of God loving the world, it was not a world of *things* but of *persons*: a world of sinners lost and ruined by the Fall, and since Christ's coming, myriads from His day to the present have believed in Him and found eternal life. As the result of Peter's preaching of Jesus of Nazareth who was slain, but whom God raised up, about 3,000 believed and were added to the church, in which all who believed had all things in common (Acts 2:41–47). Soon after, as Peter and John proclaimed Jesus and the Resurrection, the world of men was shaken, with about 5,000 of them repenting of their sin and believing the word as preached (Acts 4:4). And so the tide of salvation flowed on and on, and as Ellicott so finely put it:

> Christianity has found acceptance among widely differing nationalities. The religion of the Crucified alone among religions has a

fair claim to the title of a world-religion. Its cradle was in the East, but it rapidly found a ready acceptance in the West, and in the present-day it may be said not only to exist, but to exercise a vast and ever increasing influence in all four quarters of the globe.[1]

When Jesus was in the world, many, seeing Him in human form and listening to His fearless preaching, believed on Him. Seeing, they believed. But before He was received up into glory He said to Thomas, who asserted that "Seeing is believing" (*Except I see . . . I will not believe*), "Thomas, because thou hast seen me, thou hast believed; blessed are they that have not seen, and yet have believed" (John 20:27). In other words, *Believing is seeing.*

Since His Ascension countless myriads, whose eyes never gazed upon that radiant form of His, were saved by faith, and endured as seeing Him who is invisible. Under grace, repentant hearts are saved by *faith*—the evidence of things not seen, and as Coleridge bids us remember:

> Think not the Faith by which the Just shall live
> Is a dead creed, a map correct of Heaven,
> Far less a feeling fond and fugitive,
> A thoughtless gift, withdrawn as soon as given;
> It is an affirmation and an act
> That bids Eternal Truth by Present Fact.

It would seem as if the church has forgotten her marching orders to go out in an unbelieving world, preaching the gospel of God loving the world, Jesus dying for the sin of the world, and the Holy Spirit ever-present in the world convincing it of its sin. Is not the evangelistic spirit the emanation of the whole Godhead? The Christian church is essentially a missionary institution, with the obligation of calling upon men everywhere in the world to repent and turn to the Savior. All within her fold, who have believed on Him while in the world, should never rest until they hear other smitten souls cry, "Lord, I believe; help thou mine unbelief" (Mark 9:24). How apt are the lines of Faber:

---

[1] Ellicott, *Commentary.*

How can they live, how will they die,
How bear the cross of grief,
Who have not got the gift of faith,
The courage of belief?

Never cease to praise God, if you are among the number in this world, and the world beyond, who have believed in Him who became flesh and died for your redemption.

7

HIS GLORIFICATION

Received up into glory (1 Tim 3:16)

Among the seven pillars of divine wisdom supporting the temple of our Christian faith are those of the Incarnation and Ascension of our Lord—His descent from heaven to earth to finish the work of redemption, and then His ascent to heaven from earth as the glorious Victor, carrying with Him the triumphs of His conquest over the devil, sin, and death. The house of Dagon, god of the Philistines, was borne up by two great middle pillars, and when poor, blind Samson was brought in from prison to be made sport of, he was placed between these pillars. Taking hold of one pillar with his right hand, and the other with the left, and with God-restored muscular power, he bowed himself with all his might and crumbled those pillars as matchwood. The house quickly fell, killing 3,000 idolators beneath the heathen roof, with Samson himself perishing with his enemies.

The two massive, middle pillars upon which our spiritual house is built are eternally secure, and no Samson, religious or otherwise, can destroy the temple of truth. He came from above—He returned to His original abode—are twin facts that remain intact in spite of the apostasy of our age. The glorification of Jesus as He ascended on high was the seal of heaven that the mission He came to accomplish as He took upon Himself the likeness of our flesh was perfectly realized. Thus, as *New Testament Commentary* expresses it:

Viewed entirely, the hymn arches from Bethlehem to the heights of heavenly majesty; the Saviour is seen as the object of angelic contemplation and the subject of apostolic preaching, and He is acclaimed as the One vindicated not only in His spirit, but also in the hearts of all who believe in Him.

Therefore, one translation of this last line of the hymn has it "Who, at the end of His ministry was taken up into glory." What a blessed conclusion this is to the ancient triumph song! After thirty-three years in the far-off country of this earth of ours, in which He lived a sinless life and ultimately died for a prodigal world, Jesus returned to His Father's house, in which there was no elder brother to vent his jealousy over the loving and lavish reception accorded God's beloved Son. It was only meet that all heaven should make merry, for He, after being dead, was now alive for evermore, and was coming home a mighty Victor over His foes with the keys of death and hell dangling at His waist, trophies of His redemptive task perfectly accomplished. Now, with the hymnist, Cousins, we can sing:

To Thee, and to Thy Christ, O God
We sing, we ever sing;
For He hath crush'd beneath His rod
The world's proud rebel king.
He plunged in His imperial strength
To gulfs of darkness down
He brought his trophy up at length,
The foil'd usurper's crown.

Received up into glory. What a court reception that must have been! Who was at the gate of heaven as Jesus entered? Certainly His Father was there to welcome Him with added meaning, "This is My beloved Son, in whom I am well-pleased." It was His express desire to return to the Father and to behold the glory given Him by the Father before the world began. This is also His personal glory which the saints are to behold (John 17:25). Then all the saints of past ages before His birth (who looked for the redemption of Israel) must have been raptured as they saw Jesus and entered heaven with Him as the Redeemer efficacious to emancipate all who believe from the tyranny of their sin. If we follow the modern translation, *Taken up into glory*, the question is, Who took Him up? The moving spiritual has the stanza:

Swing low, sweet chariot—
Comin' for to carry me home;

I looked over Jordan and what did I see?
 Comin' for to carry me home.
A band of angels comin' after me—
Comin' for to carry me home.

Whatever share the angels may have in our translation to heaven,
it is evident that they were associated with Jesus in His Ascension, and
that the vast celestial host surrounding the throne of God must have
joined in the welcome their Creator received on His triumphal entry
into heaven (Ps. 24:7–10). As we have fully dealt with angelic ministration at the Ascension in PILLAR 4 under the title, "The Ascension
of Jesus," the reader is referred to this section.

Bishop Horne, in his *Commentary on the Psalms* written well over
a century ago, has this paragraph on the prophetic significance of
Psalm 68:17 where we are told, "The chariots of God are twenty
thousand, even thousands of angels . . . "

The Psalmist, in the preceding verse, had declared Sion to be the
habitation of Jehovah. In this verse is described the majesty and
appearance of His appearance there, as a mighty conqueror of the
enemies of His people, riding upon the cherubim, as in a triumphal chariot, with all the hosts of Heaven, as it were, in His retinue.
Thus God descended on Sinai with the fire, the cloud, and the
glory; thus He manifested Himself taking possession, "the holy
place," prepared for Him in Sion (2 Chron. 5:13); and in some
such manner we may suppose King Messiah to have entered
Heaven at the Ascension, when He went up in the clouds, with
power and great glory, and all the attendant spirits joined His
train, rejoicing to minister to their Lord, and increase the pomp
and splendor of that glorious day.

Our blessed assurance is that when we come to cross the swelling
tide we are to be received by Jesus Himself, as His children, as He
ushers us into His glory. Did He not promise, "I will . . . receive you
unto myself" (John 14:3)? If it is a great honor to be received at the

court of an earthly potentate or king, what an inestimable privilege it will be to be received by the King of Kings. When Stephen was dying a terrible death by stoning, he turned his bloodstained, angellike face to heaven and prayed, "Lord Jesus, receive my spirit," and after praying for those who had murdered him he fell asleep (Acts 7:54–60).

A remarkable feature of Stephen's last moments, as he looked steadfastly up into heaven and saw the glory of God, was the posture of his Lord for whom he was being martyred. Twice over we read that this most faithful witness beheld through the opened heavens, "Jesus *standing* on the right hand of God" (Acts 7:55,56), not *seated* on the right hand of the Father (Matt. 26:64; Mark 16:19). The newly ascended Lord was risen from His throne on which He is represented as eternally sitting, and was standing, ready with His outstretched nail-pierced hand to welcome the first martyr in the church He had founded into eternal bliss.

Further, Stephen saw his waiting Lord as the *Son of man*. The two references in Revelation (1:13 and 14:4) refer to a different aspect. Thus, as he looked into heaven, Stephen saw Jesus in His human form: God manifested in glorified flesh. Jesus will ever remain the perfect representative man. Dummelow, in his exposition of this title, "the Son of man," has the anonymous quotation:

> He was *the* man in whom human nature was most fully and deeply realized, and who was the most complete exponent of its capacities, warm and broad in His sympathies, ready to minister and suffer for others, sharing to the full the needs and deprivations which are the common lot of humanity, but conscious at the same time of the dignity and greatness of human nature, and destined ultimately to exalt it to unexampled majesty and glory.[1]

John Newton taught the church to sing:

> O generous love! that He, who smote
> In man the man the foe,

---

[1]Dummelow, *Commentary*, 654.

The double agony in man
For man should undergo.

We have not reached an absorbing aspect of the climax of the Incarnation, namely, our Lord's action at His Ascension, and His added relationship once back in heaven He had temporarily left in order to achieve God's redemptive plan. When Paul came to emphasize the ministry gifts of the now exalted Savior for the building up of His body, the church, He quoted the prophecy, "Thou hast ascended on high, thou hast led captivity captive; thou hast received gifts for men" (Ps. 68:18; Eph. 4:8). Arthur Way's translation of the Pauline passage reads, "He went up to Heaven's height; He led captive a train of vanquished foes; He bestowed gifts on men."

From Paradise to Heaven

What, exactly, are we to understand by the action of the Conqueror, "*he led captivity captive*" (Eph. 4:8)? That it was an action definitely related to the Ascension, is evident from the way it is connected with it. "When he ascended . . . he led . . . " The usual explanation of this phrase is that the vanquished foes of Jesus were the devil, sin, death, and the curse, which He led as a sign of His destruction of such enemies; that these were the evil principalities and powers He completely stripped of their authority by His death and resurrection, and now displayed in an open show of them (Col. 2:15). These powers of darkness had "put him to an open shame" (Heb. 6:6); and now, as Ellicott describes it, "Paul's metaphor is from a Roman triumph and represents Jesus as passing in triumphal majesty up the sacred way to the eternal gates, with the powers of evil bound as captives behind His chariot before the eyes of men and angels."

We feel, however, that there is a further aspect of this mighty Conqueror leading a band of captives vanquished by His power. Poets have loved to employ their art in describing the bliss of the one-time Paradise as if it were the promised heaven for the children of God. For instance, we have John Milton's magnificent poem, "Paradise Lost—Paradise Regained." Faber's verses on *Paradise*:

O Paradise! O Paradise!
Who doth not crave for rest?

Then Andrew Marvell in *The Garden* wrote of:

Two Paradises 'twere in one
To live in Paradise alone.

But the truth is that the *Paradise* of the New Testament was never lost and was not the sphere of eternal rest. It was not identical with heaven; nor was it a temporal abode of the saints, a kind of intermediate state where they live between their death and the coming again of Jesus to earth; neither was it a purgatory, such as the Roman Catholic Church invented in which the departed are purified or dry-cleaned before they are fit for heaven.

"Abraham's bosom" is a synonym of Paradise. Our Lord referred to it as the happy sphere where Lazarus the beggar found himself after his death (Luke 16:20–31). It was quite natural for Jews to represent Abraham as welcoming his righteous descendants to the joys of Paradise. The figure of *bosom* implies reclining next to him (see Matt. 8:11). The rich man who went to hell called on Abraham for mercy and help, but not on God to whom he could not cry.

Modern theology may maintain a seeming attitude of reverent agnosticism regarding the state of the departed, but we believe the Bible grants us sufficient light on their eternal abode and bliss. Our prayerful and careful study of Scripture prompts us to affirm that *Sheol* or its corresponding term, Hades, represented the sphere of the dead in general, and that up to the time of our Lord's Ascension this abode had its two divisions: *Paradise* for the righteous, and *hell* for all who died without God, and without hope. We believe that all in this unseen world were alive, conscious, to the full exercise of their faculties such as memory, and, as in the case of the rich man who, in spite of his wealth and lavish funeral, was in torment and concerned lest his five brothers on earth would ultimately find themselves in the same place of anguish.

The Jews taught that there were four divisions in *Sheol*:

One for those who were slain for righteousness' sake;
One for sinners who on earth had paid the penalty for their sins;

One for the just who had not suffered martyrdom;
One for sinners who had not been punished on earth.

In one of his powerful sermons, John Wesley declared, "It is plain that Paradise is not Heaven. It is indeed, if we may be allowed the expression, the *antechamber of Heaven*." The early church father, Origen, reckoned to be somewhat heterodox by the other fathers, deliberately affirmed that, "Not even the Apostles have received their early bliss, for the saints at their departure out of this life do not attain the full reward of their labours, but are awaiting us, who still remain on earth, loitering though we be but slack." Origen erred in that since the Ascension of Jesus all who die in Him do not await the final bliss of heaven.

The dying thief, believing the dying Savior to be a King, prayed that He would remember him when He came into His kingdom. What answer did Jesus give the repentant thief? He did not say, "Today shalt thou be with me in *heaven*," but "Today shalt thou be with me in *paradise*" (Luke 23:43). After their death, both went to paradise. During the three days our Lord's body was in the grave, He Himself was in paradise—and what a welcome He must have had! Could this have been the period when He preached to the spirits in their pleasant *prison*, assuring them of their release at His Ascension, and at the same time conveyed a solemn message to the doomed in hell, the other division of Sheol, regarding their ultimate abode, *the lake of fire*?

In His message of comfort to His disciples who were downcast over the information of His near death, Jesus cheered their troubled hearts, assuring them that He was going to prepare a place for them—not in *paradise*, but in the Father's spacious home—the heaven He left at His Incarnation for earth. Our ultimate destination is then eternally settled, "That where I am, there shall ye be also"—and His Ascension is the seal of such a hope. When He ascended on high, He marshaled all the saints in paradise together. As the Conqueror of Death, He led these "prisoners of hope"—the saints of past ages up to His Resurrection and Ascension who had been in a heavenly state of captivity—to heaven, God's immediate presence and their eternal abode.

In this age of grace, then, when a child of God dies, he does not go to *Abraham's bosom*, but to be with Christ, which is far better. "Absent from the body . . . present (at home) with the Lord" (2 Cor. 5:8). When Jesus entered heaven at His Ascension, He resumed His original eternal position at the Father's right hand of the majesty on high (Heb. 1:3). When Jesus returns as He said He would He will bring *all* His saints (those presently with Him) to accompany Him (1 Thess. 4:14). Positionally, we are already seated with Him in the heavenlies. A fuller treatment of the fascinating theme we have considered can be found in the author's small volume, *Death and the Life Hereafter.*

The practice application of the foregoing is not hard to make. If we profess to be *in* Christ, and already seated with Him in the heavenlies, it is incumbent upon us to seek those things which are above.

Our present attitude should be that of habitually *looking at* the Lord Jesus, what He was in His ancient glory, what He became for us as the result of His Incarnation, what He now is, and what we shall soon be with Him.

> Rise my soul, and stretch thy wings,
> Thy better portion trace;
> Rise from transitory things,
> Towards Heaven, thy native place.[2]

Men as Gifts—Gifts for Men

With His return to heaven, and to His session of power at the right hand of God, Jesus concluded all that He came to do as the God-Man, and entered upon His glorious reign over men from His throne in heaven. At his Ascension, He not only led captivity captive, but He gave men as gifts to His church, and gifts for them to use in the expansion of His church. Someone has said, "They who are ministers of His gifts are themselves gifts from Him to His church." While among his disciples Jesus revealed His wonderful design to build *His church*: "I will build my church" (Matt. 16:16–18). This magnificent expression regarding Himself occurs nowhere else in the Gospels. He called His church—*His own*—His own glorious body! He became flesh and died

---

[2] Robert Seagrove, in *The Hymnbook* (Presbyterian Church in the U.S.A., 1955), 330.

that He might bring such a church into being. In his message to the Ephesian elders, Paul urged them "to feed the church of *God*, which He hath purchased with his own blood" (Acts 20:28).

When the building is ultimately completed, Jesus will present it to Himself as "His glorious Bride, having no stain nor wrinkle, nor any such thing that she might be holy and flawless" (Eph. 5:27 *Way's Version*). The Incarnation, then, and all that was accomplished by it, became the foundation of the church Jesus said He would build, and build in such a way that the gates of hell, or powers of darkness, would never be able to prevail against it. We distinguish between the visible organization and the invisible organism. One can be a member of a church—a building or group known as such—yet not be a member of the unseen church, which is His body. The gates of hell have certainly prevailed against the church as a visible, and in many cases, a human-developed organization, hence so many branches of the Church, contrary in belief and practice. Even today "churchianity" is by "schisms rent asunder." But against *the* church He would build, no subtle, satanic force can prevail. It is important to notice that when Jesus revealed His purpose, He did not say that He would build His church on Peter, but rather upon what Peter had just confessed. The Master asked His disciple what he thought of His life and claims, and inspired by the Holy Spirit, Peter replied, "Thou art the Messiah, the Son of God"; and it is on *this* rock—Jesus as God manifested in flesh—that His church is built. Between His Resurrection and Ascension Jesus spent forty days with His chosen disciples, during which period He fully instructed them as to their share in assisting Him in the building of His church, their witness in the world, and the message they should unashamedly proclaim by the power of the Spirit (Luke 24:32–46; Acts 1:1–5).

"The promise of the Father" regarding the Holy Spirit coming upon the disciples waiting in Jerusalem was fulfilled on the historic day of Pentecost. The apostles were greatly used in the immediate enlargement of the church, when about 3,000 souls were added to it—not to a visible structure, nor to the number of disciples, but to the invisible temple, which is His body. What were the necessary qualifications for inclusion in *His* church? There had to be the glad and willing acceptance of the message Peter preached concerning Jesus as the prophesied, miracle-working, crucified, risen, and glorified Savior. There had to be a genuine and deep repentance of sin, and then baptism which represented their identification with Jesus in His death, burial, and resurrection. By these personal acts they were added to His church or joined to the Lord by the regeneration of the Spirit (Acts 2:38, 41, 47; 3:19; 4:4).

Men as Gifts

The Ascension gifts of Jesus for "building up the body of Christ" (Eph. 4:12 R.S.V.) reveal the bounty of heaven for His church on earth, and all such bestowal of these different gifts was, and is, an act of grace. "He gave"—the original pronoun *He* is emphatic, implying, He and He alone as the ascended Head and Representative of humanity. "He gave . . . apostles . . . prophets . . . evangelists . . . pastors and teachers" (Eph. 4:11, 12; 1 Cor. 12:28–31; Rom. 12:6–8). In all these references there is the same general idea, first of one body, and then of the one Spirit, guiding and animating it through various ministries. All thus chosen are gifts of the Holy Spirit. "Gift" is from an original word, *dona*, from which we get "donation"; and all the Spirit raises up for the building of the church are the donation of heaven (Heb. 2:4; James 1:17).

Gifts for Men

When He ascended on high, Jesus "gave gifts unto men" (Eph. 4:8). Having given the men, He now endows them with the necessary gifts they are to use in His service. There is, however, no uniformity about these gifts which represent a unity in diversity (Rom. 12:6; 1 Cor. 12:4–31; 14). A study of the Book of Acts reveals the nature of these manifold gifts bestowed upon men by the Lord. The greatest gift was that of the Holy Spirit, who, on the Day of Pentecost, came as the fulfillment of the promise of Jesus, "I will send My Spirit." In fact, there is a vital connection between the two declarations "I will build by church" and "I will send My Spirit." It was the coming of the Spirit that brought about the establishment and rapid enlargement of the church throughout the first century.

Then there were the gifts of power, of boldness, of faith, of wisdom, of tongues, of the ability to preach and teach, and the ability to suffer. All of the gracious gifts of the Spirit, however, for the perfecting of believers, and carrying out the administration-work of His church, and the building up of Messiah's body, are at the disposal of all believers. As Arthur Way translates Ephesians 4:7, "Not indiscriminately, however, on each of us was bestowed the bounty of God's grace, but according to the measure of its bestowal by the Master." Then there is the further word of the apostle Paul, "Having gifts that differ according to the grace given to us, let us use them" (Rom. 12:6 R.S.V.). Peter, too, has a similar exhortation, "As every man hath received the gift (his own particular gift), even so minister the same one to another, as good stewards of the manifold grace of God" (1 Peter 4:10).

The sum total of such teaching about gifts is that every member of the body of Christ at regeneration receives a gift from the Spirit to use in all future service for the Master who redeemed him. Thus, there is no born-again child of God without a regeneration-gift of some kind. The tragedy is that so many saved by grace fail to recognize this fact and consequently go through their Christian life without using their personal gift for the edification and enrichment of other believers, and for the evangelization of the lost.

Is this not the tenor of our Lord's teaching in the parable of the talents (Matt. 25:14–30), or the parable of the pounds (Luke 19:12–27)? The man with only one talent hid it in the earth, while the many with only one pound wrapped it up in a napkin. All the others, more gifted, used all they had received, wisely and well, and were thus rewarded. But the men with the one talent, or pound, failing to put it to good use, lost it. So it was a case of use it, or lose it. These parables depict the action of those who shut up their gifts from the active service of Christ, and so retard the progress of the gospel in a world of need. Where are *you*, personally, in this matter? Have you discovered your regeneration-gift, or gifts, and are you employing them to the full for the glory of Him who bestowed them? Or can it be, *God forbid*, that since your salvation, which was a gift of grace, your particular gift has been buried in the napkin of neglect? If so, then you will suffer loss when Jesus comes to reward His servants for the use of all He made possible for them. Failure to employ your gift will not mean the loss of eternal life, but of the crown of life promised to all who are faithful in life and stewardship.

Bishop Horne fittingly summarizes the truths just considered in his paraphrase of Ephesians 4:8:

Thou, O Christ, who didst descend from the right hand of the Majesty in the heavens, to the lowest parts of the earth, art again ascended to the right hand of the Majesty in the heavens: "Thou hast led captivity captive"; Thou hast conquered the conqueror bound the strong one, redeemed human nature from the grave, and triumphantly carried it, with Thee, to the throne of God: "Thou hast received gifts for men," yea, for the rebellious also; and being thus ascended to Glory, Thou hast received of the Father the promise of the Spirit, with all His gifts and graces, to bestow upon the sons of men, even upon such as heretofore have not only broken Thy laws, but appeared in arms against Thee; yet of such as these, converted by the power of the Gospel, wilt Thou form and establish a Church, "that the Lord Thy God may dwell among them;" that so, of Thy faithful people, gathered from all parts of the world, may be built up a living temple, "a habitation of God through the Spirit."

Composition of Trinity Changed

It is not generally understood that Jesus' return to Glory, as the Man of Sorrows acquainted with human grief (whom angels acclaimed at His Ascension) brought about a change in the composition of the Trinity, which before the Incarnation was made up of God who is Spirit; The Holy Spirit, and God the Son—all Three having the same essence, the same elements of personality, but devoid of a person, or body, such as God the Son assumed when He left heaven and became the Son of Man. What form their eternal essence was clothed with, we are not told!

But this we do know, that with Christ's Ascension and return to the Holy Cabinet, there is a Member of it who, although He became God manifested in the flesh, and the One who was touched with the feeling of human infirmities, went back to heaven as the One well-qualified to assume the office of the Great High Priest, to make intercession for those humans on earth with whom He was closely identified. No wonder the angelic host, and likewise the redeemed host in glory, exclaim, "Worthy is the Lamb that was slain." The Trinity now has a God in glorified human form, and thus it is encouraging to our faith, as we linger amid the shadows, to know that we have an Advocate at the right hand of God who was tempted in all points as we are, but who was victorious, and who is ever ready to make us the recipients of His victory.

God with a Human Face

While a prisoner of Jehoiachin held captive by the river Chebar, Ezekiel had visions of God as the heavens opened. His captivity did not prevent him receiving a captivating revelation of the glory of God. Among the visions granted the imprisoned prophet was that of "the likeness of the throne (and) . . . the appearance of a man above upon it" (Ezek. 1:26). How prophetic this vision was of the glorified humanity of the Man Christ Jesus after His return to heaven to assume dominion of all things.

What must be borne in mind is the fact that it was no new experience for angels to watch saints enter heaven with the human bodies in which they had died, but transformed in their ascent to the abode of God and the angels. Both Enoch and Elijah were translated directly without tasting death. Both Moses and Elijah came to the Mount of Transfiguration, in their glorified but recognizable bodies. The Babe born at Bethlehem (who became the man crucified at Calvary) was *God* manifested in the flesh, and the wonder among the angels, who before had never looked on God, was to see God the Son for the first time, and that with a human face.

To the celestial host it was the marvel of marvels to see those hands once pierced with nails, now holding the sceptre of authority, ruling over all, and having all events under His control. They also saw those human feet once nailed to a bloody cross, representing the purchase price of His saving grace, and thus turned their harps to praise Him. Through all eternity the object of universal worship and adoration in heaven will be that of the wonderful sight of humanity's dust, glorified, and seated on a throne.

Till God in human flesh I see,
My thoughts no comfort find:
The holy, just, and sacred THREE,
Are terrors to my mind.
But if EMMANUEL's face appear,
My soul surmounts each slavish fear.

Who and what Jesus is in heaven brings us to a consideration of His intimate identification with our humanity and with human relationship in respect to His own. As our Emmanuel, *God with us*, He is now *God for us*, exercising His mediatorial character and fulfilling His high prophetical, priestly, and royal offices for the welfare of His church and the world.

Oh teach us, Lord, to know and own
This wondrous mystery,
That Thou in Heaven with us art one,
And we are one with Thee.

Growing up in a typical godly Jewish home, Jesus came to know all about human relationship, seeing He was brought up with brothers and sisters born to Joseph and Mary after His own wondrous birth. Thus, when He entered His public ministry at about thirty years of age and gathered disciples around Him, in a most effective way He spiritualized these close associations of home life. So we find Him calling all who obeyed the will of His Father in heaven, His *brothers* and *sisters*; and all who followed His commands, His *friends* (Matt. 12:50; John 15:14, 15).

Now that Jesus Himself is in heaven, He does not receive us as His mean subjects, but as those who have a blood relationship with Him brought about through His sacrifice on our behalf. Has the reality of this privileged association gripped *your* heart? Think of it, he calls you *brother* or *sister*. Why should we charge our hearts with unnecessary care and concern when we have in Jesus One who wears our nature, whose heart beats in union with ours, and whose brotherly love toward us never fails? During the widespread famine in Egypt Joseph supplied his brothers with all they needed, and our heavenly Joseph's fraternal kindness ever corresponds to our need. As we approach the throne of grace, then, let us remember that our Brother occupies it, and that He will withhold no good thing from us.

> Our nearest Friend, our Brother now,
> Is He to whom the angels bow;
> They join with us to praise His name,
> But we the nearest interest claim.

He is, indeed, "our nearest Friend," the Friend who loveth at all times and sticketh closer than a brother; and the One who bears our sins and griefs and to whom we can take everything in prayer. And His friendly ability to help us is one of the joys that was set before Him when He endured the cross and despised its shame. Closely allied to the consoling personal associations of Jesus with those who are His as members of His body (of which He is Head) are those of a more official character whom the New Testament lists as He was received up into glory.

Forerunner

Commenting on this title, found only in Hebrews 6:20, Professor A.B. Bruce says that it "expresses the whole essential difference between the Christian and Levitical religion—between the religion that brings men nigh to God, and the religion that kept or left men standing afar off." The Jewish High Priest entered the Holy Place by himself, one day in the year, but only as the people's representative, not as a *forerunner* for any who might dare follow him. When Jesus entered the Holy of Holies at His Ascension, He went beyond the Veil as our *Forerunner*, and likewise as our *Leader*, by His own blood, taking us there with Him (Heb. 9:24; 10:19). Before He left His own, He assured them that He was going to prepare a place for them (John 14:2, 3).

In classical usage, *forerunner* implies "One who goes before, as a scout to reconnoiter, or as a herald to announce the coming of a king, or to make ready the way for a royal journey." While we use the term *forerunner* of John the Baptist, the Gospels do not describe him as such, but as the *messenger* sent "before thy (the Lord's) face," and to "prepare thy way," and to exhort the people to make "his paths straight" (Luke 3:4; 7:27). Thus, John was in a true sense his Lord's forerunner, just as

Jesus was the Baptist's *Forerunner* into the Most Holy Place. Going before His own into the heavenly abode, Jesus had no need to reconnoiter it as a scout, seeing that He had lived there through the past eternity, before His Incarnation. He was the One who went before to announce His greatest victory, to open the way for the blood-washed to enter the holiest of all, and to act as their Representative.

Mediator

This further expressive metaphor applied to the exalted Savior occurs twice in the New Testament, first of Moses as the mediator of the Law (Gal. 3:19, 20), then of Jesus as the "one mediator between God and men," and as the Mediator of a "better" or "new" covenant (1 Tim. 2:5; Heb. 8:6; 9:15; 12:24). Throughout Scripture, mediation, in which God deals with man, or man with God, not directly, but through the interposition of another, is fairly common. In intercessory prayer, such mediation is the privilege of all the saints (James 5:16).

Mediator is from a root meaning "middle," and such a person in certain human relationships is the middle man, the go-between, who intervenes between two parties for peace and unites parties at variance. Jesus is our Middle-Man who presents our prayers, our praises, our persons to God though Himself. In the use of the term as applied to Jesus there was never, and cannot ever be, any disagreement on God's side to appease and make amenable to man. Variances to deal with are all on the human side. As the embodiment of God's mediating oath, Jesus "confirmed it with an oath" (Heb. 6:17). Is this not our plea at the throne of grace, our song in the house of our pilgrimage, and our confidence in the prospect of death—that Jesus is our Mediator?

Because of His holiness and righteousness, God must ever be the eternal enemy of sin. As the abominable thing He hates, He can never be reconciled to sin, but He looks upon it with abhorrence. How then can He receive, bless, and commune with sinners like ourselves? Only through a Mediator, and Jesus, as the Son of God, knows all about the divine side, and ever honors all the Father's perfections. Then as the One who became the Son of Man, He knows all that there is to know from the human side. He makes man acceptable to God through His own glorious righteousness and finished work of redemption.

The "*daysman* betwixt us," Job wrote of that one who "lay his hand upon us both" (9:33), the litigants, "in token of his power to adjudicate between them," is akin to an "umpire" or "mediator." The only *umpire* to whose authoritative decision both God and ourselves are equally amenable is the *God-Man*, who is on a level with God and man. He never fails to reconcile the repentant, believing sinner to God. On God's part, He has no need of reconciliation to man (1 Tim. 2:5). Sinners can only be reconciled to Him through the death of His Son.

Advocate

A further feature of our ascended Lord's ministry in heaven is that of *advocacy*—"We have an advocate with the Father, Jesus Christ the righteous" (1 John 2:1). The simple, original meaning of "advocate" is that of one called to help, or one who pleads in favor of and is the representative of another. This term is likewise applied to the Holy Spirit and is translated in the A.V. as *Comforter* (John 14:26; 15:26; 16:7). All the ideas included in this office apply *both* to the Holy Spirit and to Jesus. Since an *advocate* is one who pleads in favor of and is the representative of another, we are doubly blessed in our twin Divine Advocates. Away back in Job, the word before us carried the twofold meaning of one who comforts or exhorts and one is who is appealed to, as a proxy or attorney, or one called to our aid (Job 16:2).

In the goodness of God we have two wonderful Advocates, for the ideas associated with such an office apply both to the Lord Jesus and to the Holy Spirit. During His earthly ministry Jesus was God's Advocate with men, pleading God's cause with them and seeking to win them for Him. Now He is our Advocate in heaven, for by His sacrifice He returned to heaven there to appear in the presence of God *for us*, pleading for us against every argument of Satan. "He ever lives to make intercession for us" (Heb. 7:25). Ellicott's comment on 1 John 2:1, "We have an Advocate with the Father," is enlightening:

> The Redeemer, the Word made flesh, and re-ascended with His human nature, is that part of the deity which assures us of the ever-active vitality of divine love. If the justice of God is connected most with the Father, then mercy is pledged by the Son. He has exalted our nature, undertaken our interests, presented our

prayers, and will one day be surrounded by the countless million of His human brothers whom He has rescued, wearing the same nature as Himself. He is represented as continuing our Advocate, because otherwise, His work might appear a separate earthly manifestation: *righteous* because Christ, the only blameless example of human nature, can alone intercede with God, Heb. 7:26; 1 Peter 3:18; John 16:8–10.[3]

It is thus that we can sing with loving, grateful hearts:

Look up, my soul, with cheerful eye:
See where the great Redeemer stands,
The glorious Advocate on high,
With precious incense in His hands;
And on His pleading still depend,
Who is thy Advocate and Friend.

But as Jesus was about to leave His disciples and ultimately return to heaven, He did not want to leave them as *orphans*, or as the R.V. translates "comfortless." So He promised, "I will pray the Father, and he shall give you another Comforter (Advocate) . . . even the Spirit of truth" (John 14:16, 17). It is interesting to observe that the simple word *another* has a twofold implication in the original, namely:

1. One of the same kind, and

2. Another of a different kind.

Needless to say, it is the first meaning that Jesus used, and it suggests that He would send another Comforter like Himself who, although He would not be recognized by an unspiritual world, would yet be lovingly received by believers (John 14:16, 17, 25, 26). The Holy Spirit would constantly testify to them of their unseen Lord who, although absent in body, would still be present with them by His Spirit (John 14:16, 18).

---

[3] Ellicott, *Commentary.*

Thus the ideas embodied in *Advocate* apply both to the Spirit and to the Savior. As the latter intercedes with God *for* us above, the Spirit intercedes *in us* below (Rom. 8:26, 34; Heb. 7:25). By this means, although Jesus is no longer on earth, as the Holy Spirit is His Spirit, absent in body, He is still with us. We have the Advocate within to convict us when sin is committed, and another Advocate in heaven to plead His efficacious blood on our behalf.

> Christ is our Advocate on high,
> Thou art our Advocate within!
> Oh, plead the truth, and make reply,
> To every argument of sin.

T. Binney, in his awe-inspiring hymn, "Eternal Light! Eternal Light!," has the most impressive verse:

> There is a way for man to rise
> To that sublime abode;
> An Offering and a Sacrifice,
> A Holy Spirit's energies,
> An Advocate with God.

Priest

Received up into glory, our Savior entered upon His priestly ministry, which has continued for almost two millennia. It will not cease until His church is raptured. He is now our Great High Priest who passed into the heavens to plead His sacrificial death on our behalf, to make intercession for us, and to sympathize, succor and sanctify His redeemed ones. Because of His willingness to become manifest in flesh, He became vitally associated with many human infirmities, and He is thus able to present our cause. As our priestly Intercessor, Jesus is ever willing to make requests of the Father on our behalf, on the basis of His perfect sacrifice for our salvation (Heb. 4:14, 15; 9:31; 1 Peter 3:22).

Because He is alive forevermore, His people share his risen life, and in glory He sees the limit of the travail of His soul while on earth, in the regeneration, sanctification, perseverance, and glorification of all those in His beloved family. As their Priest, He lives to pray for them, console with them, and watch over them. He lives to execute all the purposes of the Father concerning the church He purchased with His blood to be representatives of His holiness.

Further, when He entered upon His priestly ministry, it was not to create a priesthood within His church, or to have its individual ministers as *priests*, but that *all* true believers should become "kings and priests unto God" (Rev. 5:10); or "a kingdom and priests to our God" (Rev 5:10 R.S.V.); "a royal priesthood" (1 Peter 2:9); "a holy priesthood" (1 Peter 2:5). Thus, the Old Testament revelation that Israel was "a kingdom of priests unto God" was transferred to the spiritual Israel, the church, under the New Dispensation. As the Glorified Christ is princely as well as priestly, all of His own are to share in His dominion over the earth.

It is to be questioned, however, if all the children of God on this side of heaven realize their priceless position and privileges as a company of worshipping priests, namely, that they can have boldness to enter the holiest of all by a new and living way through the veil; that they have direct access to the Father by the Spirit; that theirs is the responsibility of offering up both *spiritual* and *living* sacrifices (Heb. 10:19–22; 1 Peter 2:5, 6); and also to offer up prayers and praises (Heb. 13:15; Rev. 8:3).

King

Not only is Jesus in glory, "the head of the church" (Eph. 5:23), those hands of His, once pierced by nails, now hold the sceptre of universal empire. All power in heaven and on earth is His. "The government" is "upon his shoulder" (Isa. 9:6); He has "the keys of hell and of death" (Rev. 1:18); and thus "he . . . openeth, and no man shutteth; and shutteth, and no man openeth" (Rev. 3:7). By him, the crucified King, "kings reign, and princes decree justice" (Prov. 8:15), and "he removeth kings, and setteth up kings: he giveth wisdom unto the wise" (Dan. 2: 21).

When He returns to earth, in its length and breadth it will be the seat of His kingdom as He fashions the kingdoms of this world into the kingdoms of His own, and of His Father. What a blissful era that will be when every enemy shall be put under His feet. The loving hand of Jesus, raised in blessing over the head of His children, now controls every event. This is man's day, and the world appears to be generally Christless, yet He rules over it by His power; He rules in the church by His Word; He rules in the heart of the believer by His Spirit. Amid all that oppresses and depresses, the triumph of faith is—*He reigneth*.

His kingdom cannot fail;
He rules o'er earth and Heaven;
The keys of death and hell
Are to our Jesus given:
Lift up your heart, lift up your voice,
Rejoice, aloud, ye saints, rejoice![4]

There are those who affirm that nowhere in Scripture is Jesus called *King* of His followers. In reply to that accusation attention is drawn to the phrase in Revelation 15:3, "Thou King of saints," or "King of nations" (as the marginal reading suggests). How we love the phrase, "Thou King of saints," and how we sing, "The King of Love my Shepherd is." True, He was born King of the Jews, and when they rejected Him and cried out for His death, Pilate asked, "Shall I crucify your king?" The question was asked, "Art thou a king then?" and Jesus answered, "To this end was I born" (John 18:33–37).

But while much of the Kingship of Jesus relates to Jacob (who received the term *Israel* after he was circumcised and then it was consistently applied to Jacob's descendants, see Luke 1:33), Abraham became the father of all who believed, and so Paul affirms that all who are "Christ's" are "Abraham's seed" (Gal. 3:29). In Romans 9:6 Paul also speaks of two Israels: "For they are not all Israel (that is *spiritual*), which are of Israel" *natural* Israel). Those Jews who continued to offer sacrifices in the temple were "Israel after the flesh" (1 Cor. 10:18). But spiritual Jews believing in Christ for salvation were the true Israel of God (1 Cor. 10:18) and members of His church, who recognized and revered His reign over their lives.

All believers, born anew by the Holy Spirit, whether Jews or Gentiles, are saints, but some are more saintly than others, and the

---

[4]Charles Wesley, "We Come, Oh Christ, To Thee" in *The Hymnbook*, 140.

difference in the degree of practical sanctification is allied to the Lordship, or Kingship, of Jesus, in heart and life. When He is given the throne of a life, of the increase of His rule in such a life, there is no end, for the path of such a saint shines more and more unto the perfect day. The personal question is, "If you claim to be a Christian, have you given your Savior His coronation as King over all that you are and have?" Remember, He was born, not only as *Savior*, but as *Christ the Lord*!

8

THE FUNDAMENTAL AND SPIRITUAL VALUE OF THE INCARNATION

Under this last section of our sacred meditation we come to realize that the more closely the virgin birth of our Lord is studied, the more clearly will it be seen that it involves in a most vital and central way the entire doctrine of the Incarnation.

There are those who would have us believe that the virgin birth has no important doctrinal value connected with it, and that belief in it is not to be regarded as essential to the acceptance of the Christian faith. As Professor Orr so tersely puts it: "It is a fair question to ask whether the Virgin Birth of the Lord took place or not. If it did not, there is an end of the matter. But it is impossible to doubt that, if it did take place, if this was the way in which God actually brought His Only-Begotten into the world—then it is vitally connected in some way with the fact of the Incarnation, and cannot be treated with indifference."[1]

But that absolute faith in the verity of our Lord's virgin birth is imperative will now be our purpose to prove.

The Virgin Birth Is the Foundation of the Gospel

The superb structure of the life and character of our Lord Jesus Christ has, as its immovable and only foundation, His virgin birth.

---

[1] Orr, The Virgin Birth.

Other foundation can no man lay, and yet retain the Savior whom the Bible portrays.

If Christ was born of human parents, or in other words, if there was noting miraculous about His birth such as being conceived by the Holy Ghost suggests, or if the New Testament narratives are not genuine but full of mistakes, or of deliberate, intentional fabrication, or of mythical folklore, then we are shut up to one or two very solemn and tragic conclusions.

(a) If Jesus was not conceived by the Holy Ghost, and born of a virgin, then Mary's character is blasted, and her Child stamped as the offspring of lust and shame, for He was born out of wedlock.

(b) If Jesus was not conceived by the Holy Ghost and born of a virgin then He is not the Holy One whom we believe Him to be, for never in the history of mankind has natural generation produced a sinless being. Rejection of Christ's holy birth means the rejection of His holy spotless life. As the late Prof. A.B. Bruce said, "With the denial of the Virgin Birth is apt to go denial of the Virgin Life."

"Doctrinally," says Professor Orr, "it must be repeated that the belief in the Virgin Birth of Christ is of the highest value for the right apprehension of Christ's unique and sinless personality. Here is One, as Paul brings out in Romans 5:12, who, free from sin Himself, and not involved in the Adamic liabilities of the race, reverses the curse of sin and death brought in by the first Adam, and establishes the reign of righteousness and life. Had Christ been naturally born, not one of these things could be affirmed of Him. As one of Adam's race, not an entrant from a higher sphere, He would have shared in Adam's corruption and doom—would Himself have required to be redeemed. Through God's infinite mercy, He came from above, inherited no guilt, needed no regeneration of sanctification, but became Himself the Redeemer, Regenerator, Sanctifier, for all who receive Him."[2] "Thanks be unto God for his unspeakable gift" (2 Cor. 9:15). And well might we sing, "Hallelujah! What a Saviour."

(c) If Jesus was not conceived by the Holy Ghost and born of a virgin, then how are we to account for His supernatural claims, and the unparalleled and undying influence for truth and goodness He has

---

[2] Ibid.

exerted in the history of the race? If we deny His supernatural birth, then we reject His supernatural Person and work. And this is a distinguishing mark of all those who do reject the virgin birth, that they have not an adequate view of the Lord, but hold a lowered view, calling Him "Jesus" merely, and referring to Him as "The Peasant of Galilee" and other such appellations.

(d) If Jesus was not conceived by the Holy Ghost, and born of a virgin, then He was not the preexistent One, and He lied when He said, "Before Abraham was, I am." For as we have already shown, a natural birth marks the beginning of a new life, a life that had no separate existence before.

If, as the critics allege, the narratives, or some of the texts within the narratives, are not to be relied upon, then the whole system of doctrine that the New Testament contains is built upon a false foundation. What becomes of inspiration and of the Scriptures being the Revelation of the mind and will of God, if we tamper thus with any part of them?

There remain one or two minor applications that can be fitly placed under the fundamental value of the virgin birth because they form an important part of its outcome.

The Virgin Birth Is a Figure of Regeneration

It must be evident to every spiritually-minded believer that the mystery of the virgin birth of our Lord is akin to the new birth of the sinner. Take for instance passages like:

John 1:13—"Which were born . . . of God"

John 3:6—"That which is born of the Spirit is spirit"

1 Peter 1:22–23—"Through the Spirit . . . being born again"

And what do we find within such? Why, just as our Lord was born of the Holy Ghost and thereby received another nature, namely, a human one, so the sinner is born again by the same Spirit and receives as a consequence a new nature, namely, a divine one. A sinner becomes a Christian by conception of the Holy Spirit, thereby making every Christian a miniature incarnation.

It is because Christ took our flesh, and was born of a virgin, that He can be spiritually born in our hearts. And what will it profit us that Christ was born into the world unless He can be born in our hearts? Yes, and once we experience the Holy Spirit's work of regeneration there is no difficulty regarding the virgin birth! Why, it is the fact of the virgin birth that gives power to the appeal for man's regeneration.

"If we realize," says Prebendary Sadler, "that He who died to save us is God Incarnate, we never can be tormented with doubts about the ability and willingness to save, or whether we have an interest in Him. We are raised into an atmosphere above all this.

"Able to save you?—Why, He is your God.
"Willing to save you?—Why, He took your flesh for this one purpose."

What must never be forgotten is the glorious fact that the devil is a defeated foe, and that the Victor ever is at hand to share His triumph with us. As the poet Cousins has portrayed the conquest:

... His glorious arm the strife maintained,
He march'd in might from far;
His robes were with the vintage stained,
Red with the wine of war. . . .

To Thee, and to Thy Christ, O God,
We sing, and ever sing;
For He hath crush'd beneath His rod
The world's proud rebel king.
He plunged in His imperial strength
To gulfs of darkness down,
He brought His trophy up at length,
The foil'd usurper's crown.
Well might we sing then, "Thanks be unto God, who giveth us the victory!"

Yes, the virgin birth is both the figure and the pledge of Regeneration; thus with true hearts we sing the carol:

Mild He lays His glory by,
Born that man no more may die,
Born to raise the sons of earth,
Born to give them second Birth.

And yet the tragedy of it all is that although Christ's Virgin Birth gives such efficacy to the blood that He shed, an efficacy which can be experienced only by those who trust it, so many fail to believe such a stupendous fact. Indeed, one can detect the shadow of Calvary gathered round Bethlehem that night our Lord was born. "The little village of the least of the tribes said truly it had no room for the Immense and the Incomprehensible. There was an unconscious truth even in its inhospitality. And," as F. W. Faber goes on to say, "as He was born outside the walls of Bethlehem, so must He die outside the walls of Jerusalem. Alas! the spirit of Bethlehem is but the spirit of a world which has forgotten God! . . . Bethlehem is what the Creator does to His creatures; Calvary is what His creatures do to Him."

The Virgin Birth Is a Foreshadowing of Sanctification

Keeping in mind the outstanding features of our Lord's virgin birth, can we not understand more fully the doctrine of sanctification as we have it in Paul's mystic phrase of Galatians 4:19, "I travail in birth again until Christ be formed in you"? Many things are beyond the range of our vision in connection with the virgin birth, but these factors are open to us, namely, Mary's faith and self-surrender, and on the other hand the operation of the Holy Spirit. And Paul's desire for the believers at Galatia, which is but an echo of the inner message of the virgin birth, is that the reincarnation of Christ is possible only when we have Mary's self-surrender and faith, and when, like her, we allow the Holy Spirit to produce Christ in and through us. The treasure of heavenly glory must now be seen in earthly vessels. As God was seen in Christ, so now Christ must be seen in us.

With the countenance of Man, and the character of God, Jesus could affirm, "He that hath seen me, hast seen the Father (John 14:9). Those who crave a more present, immediate manifestation of God must realize that no further revelation is to be made because one is not needed, nor could be made. God has displayed in Christ *all* He desired man to see. Thus, in effect, Jesus said, "There is no more of the Father you can see than you have seen in me. The Father, Himself, is in me, speaking and acting among you through me." Nature reveals God's power, but is silent as to His grace and truth—which attributes came in His beloved Son. Deity, in itself, is invisible. "No man hath seen God at any time." Yet, when clothed with humanity He shines through gloriously.

Can we humbly confess, "He that hath seen *me* hath seen the Saviour? Is it not the incarnate ministry of the Holy Spirit, who brought about the fusion of deity and humanity in one Person, the Lord Jesus Christ, to produce Christlikeness in our character and conduct so that we, too, can confess with Paul, "I live, yet not I, Christ liveth in me?" We need Him in us reproducing His own life, even as He lived it out among men, just as much as we need His death for us. Sanctity of heart is simply the manifestation of Jesus in the life of a child of God.

> Not I, but Christ, be honoured, loved, exalted,
> Not I, but Christ, be seen, be known, and heard:
> Not I, but Christ, in ev'ry look and action,
> Not I, but Christ, in every thought and word.

The truth we must more intelligently and experientially grasp is our complete identification with our Lord who became the Word made flesh: who was crucified and buried as our Substitute; but who rose again and ascended on high as our Representative. He died that we might live through, by, and for Him. As He died for us, we must die to sin; as He rose again to plead our cause, we have been raised in Him; as He entered heaven, as our Forerunner, our thoughts, hopes, and affections should ascend heavenward. Ascended and reigning, Jesus manages our affairs, fulfills His promises on our behalf, and is preparing for us a dwelling place in the Father's house. Now above the world, He looks to us to share His ascended life, and live above the vanities, amusements, and policies of this present world so dead in sin.

In Mary's submission of her body, yes, and of her reputation also for the time being, we see the only pathway to a life that is radiant with the image of our Lord. Let us look in closing at her word of full acquiescence regarding the divine will. Here are her beautiful words, breathing it would seem the very air of Gethsemane and Calvary: "Behold the handmaid of the Lord, be it unto me according to thy word" (Luke 1:38). The word "handmaid" we are told is *doulee* signifying "the female slave." There are two messianic Psalms where the phrase "The son of thine handmaid" occurs (Ps. 86:16; 116:16). And in both instances the word "handmaid" means the same thing, namely, "the female slave."

And such a word not only reveals the depths of humiliation that our Lord descended to when He became the Son of God's female slave; it also speaks to us of Mary's entire surrender to the Lord. She called herself the slave of the Lord! And as a slave she made her body not her own but her Master's, and thus, to Him it was surrendered in full and glad obedience.

Beloved, before the reader and the writer of this book part company, shall we not put this question to our separate hearts: "Am I willing to become the slave of the Lord in order that Christ may be formed in me?" Are we prepared to follow Mary in her blissful submission and say: "Behold the female (or male) slave of the Lord; be it unto me according to Thy word"? Can we each say, as we bow silently before "Our Glorious Victor, Prince Divine," that we are "glad vassals of a Saviour's throne"? If we can, then we have caught the inner meaning of the virgin birth, and the Holy Ghost will assuredly overshadow us, even as He did the virgin, and extract the dross from the silver until in all our ways, thoughts, and words, Christ is formed.

And so at the end of our meditation upon such a sacred theme we return to our opening thought; that is—the holy, virgin life of the believer is necessary if the virgin birth of our Lord is to be rightly comprehended. And not only so, it is the constant presence of Christ within us that keeps our lives like His own. Or as Watson in his *Body of Divinity* would have us remember: "As Christ was conceived in the womb of a virgin, so, if He be born in thee, thy heart is a virgin-heart in respect of sincerity and sanctity. Art thou purified from the hold of sin? If Christ be born in thy heart, it is a *Sanctum Sanctorum*, a holy of holies. If thy heart be polluted with the predominant love of sin, never think Christ is born there. Christ will never lie any more in a stable. If He be born in thy heart, it is consecrated by the Holy Ghost." And with such a spiritual application John the Apostle agrees when he declares that "Whatsoever is begotten of God sinneth not" (1 John 5:4, 19).

Such is God's ideal for your life and mine, and it can be blessedly realized as the result of the virgin birth of our Lord. How shall we respond? As only as we can if we want God's best as James Montgomery expresses it:

Thou with the gift of holiness within us;
We not less human, but made more divine,
Our lives replete with Heaven's supernal beauty,
Ever declare that beauty, Lord, is Thine.